ALGARVE

Text by
Conceição Branco

EIB
BONECHI

© Copyright by Casa Editrice Bonechi - Florence - Italy E-mail: bonechi@bonechi.it - Internet: www.bonechi.it www.bonechi.com

Printed in Italy by Centro Stampa Editoriale Bonechi.

Photographs from the Archives of Casa Editrice Bonechi taken by Paolo Giambone *with the exception of those on pages:*
4, 7 below, 13, 20, 28 above, 42 above, 44 below, 58, 88 below, 93 above, taken by Jean Charles Pinheira;
12, 22, 25, 28 below, 29, 30 above, 32, 44 above, 51 above, 70, 81 above, 88, 89, 90, 91, 92, taken by Zimmerling.

ISBN 88-8029-089-4

Traditional donkey cart

INTRODUCTION

*T*he Algarve is a land of contrasts, of sheer rock and rolling hills, deserted beaches and towns of white-walled houses which tumble to the sea. On the sotavento, or leeward shore, there are long beaches with dunes of fine sand, while on the barlavento, to windward, there are sandy coves like shells ringed by cliffs of red earth. North, along routes which Romans, Arabs and many other peoples have followed over the centuries, lies the lush green of the serra. To the northeast rise the harsh uplands which border the Alentejo. It is a land of rivers too, separated from Andalusia and the Spanish by the gleaming waters of the Guadiana which stretch out unbroken as far as the eye can see.

From the Guadiana to the ocean extends the land known as the Al-Garb. The name, which simply means "the west", was coined by the Arabs, whose links with the region as both traders and conquerors date back to the eighth century. Won over by its warm sunshine, golden sand and delightful scenery, the Arabs turned the Algarve into a playground for the rich and powerful, a place for philosophers to meditate and poets to dream.

In earlier times, long before the Arabs came to power, the Romans were seduced by the region's charms. For the legions which marched down from the north, the Algarve set a southern limit on their conquests. Weary of fighting, they put aside their weapons and built sumptuous villas, public baths and factories to cure seafood caught in the waters off the coast, which they sent to furnish the banqueting tables of Imperial Rome

Later the Lusitanian people followed the path first traced by the Romans to establish the borders which Portugal, one of Europe's oldest nations, retains to this day.

All these changes did nothing to dim the attractions

of the Algarve, which the Portuguese crown regained from the Arabs in the thirteenth century. It was in Sagres, described by the poet Luís de Camões as the place where land ends and sea begins, that Henry the Navigator, son of King João I, dreamt of opening up new routes around the world. To make his vision a reality, the first caravels set off from the port of Lagos five hundred years ago on voyages of exploration, which would bring Europeans to lands and peoples they had only imagined.

Traditionally a melting pot of different cultural influences, the Algarve remains a welcoming destination for travellers, a crossroads for people from all over the world and the perfect place to take it easy and enjoy life.

The people of the Algarve like to linger out of doors in the cool of the evening, chatting, or admiring the subtle, changing tones of sunset. Food figures prominently in their conversation, and their cuisine features a judicious mixture of flavours and colours from the mountains and the sea. Evening get-togethers often carry on long into the night and, as they themselves put it, they "welcome those who come with good intentions".

In the Algarve, the locals know how to have a good time and traditional dances can be wild and energetic. In the corridinho the girls wear balloon skirts which reveal glimpses of lace underwear as they skip ever faster through their steps. The men, straight backed and severe, move only their feet, keeping time with the band leader and the music of the concertina.

They enjoy keeping alive the legends of the past, and their folk tales are full of brave sailors, Roman centurions, turbaned arabs and mouras encantadas - enchanted mooresses or magical sprites said to live in rivers and wells.

Every year in spring, when the blossom falls from the almond trees and covers the fields in a blanket of white they tell the story of a nordic princess who came to the Algarve to marry the King of the Moors and who was overcome with homesickness for the frozen wastes of her own country. Her husband, who loved her very much, grew sadder and sadder,

and with him his subjects, who were normally happy and contented. The king called a meeting of all the wisest men in his kingdom and together they found a solution. Following their advice, the king ordered thousands of almond trees to be planted on the hills around the palace. Eventually a day came when the princess opened the windows of the palace and, finding the trees covered in white flowers tinged with pink, believed she was seeing the snows of her homeland again. Her melancholy was cured and the people of the kingdom, amazed at her recovery and glad to see their rulers back in good spirits, planted almond trees in all their fields. Perhaps they hoped the trees would have asimilar effect on them, for even now there are few gardens and courtyards where the windows don't look down onto an almond tree.

There is another version of this legend which the writer José Saramago claims to have found when he was seeking the reason for another of the Algarve's customs. In this variant the princess fell so ill pining for the snows of her homeland that the king feared for her life. As the palace stood in a large town, like Faro or Silves perhaps, it was surrounded by houses the colour of earth or clay, as the locals liked them. There wasn't the smallest splash of white to be seen anywhere.

So the king decreed that all the houses should be white-washed at the same time on the same day. When the princess came to the window she found the whole town covered in white. Because the walls stayed white, unlike the blossom which fell and gave way to fruit, the princess could look out whenever she wanted, and she soon got better.

To this day, houses in the Algarve are never painted any colour but white. To indulge their creativity people in the Algarve started the tradition of wide stucco decorated mouldings, known as platibandas. And they also kept narrow bands of colour to mark the edges of walls: yellows, to ward off evil, and blues to attract benevolent spirits and bring happiness.

Throughout the Algarve, old traditions mingle with more cosmopolitan ways of life in a landscape of outstanding natural beauty.

West Coast beaches

ALJEZUR

Here the sun takes leave of the land, dipping into the wide Atlantic. Down in one of the sandy coves the day dies to the sound of the swell and the flight of seagulls. Inland, towns nestle in the folds of hills, leaving the wide spaces to the shrill wind, fresh with the scent of wild flowers.

Along the road which snakes from Lagos to Aljezur, the silence is broken only by birdsong and calling crows. Arriving in the town itself, the first sight is the castle brooding on the hilltop. The houses in the old town run in lines strung between two hills, **Degoladoira** (The Axeman's Hill) and **Cabeças** (Heads). Grim reminders of the XIII century, when Christian troops stormed the castle and took the town.Seawards, the houses crouch low on the land. At Arrifana, the picturesque fishing harbour is fronted by a rock known as **Ponta da Agulha** (Needle Point) which rises above the beach. A lazy day trip here can take you on to the village of Odeceixe, past places where time has stood still.

Moorish Castle (X century)

6

VILA DO BISPO

Passing through **Vila do Bispo** on the way to Sagres, it's worth taking time to look at the octagonal tower of the **Igreja da Raposeira**, completed in the sixteenth century, and the image of Nossa Senhora da Encarnação, which dates from two centuries earlier. Nearby stands the **Ermida de Nossa Senhora de Guadelupe**, built by the Knights Templar in the thirteenth century.

One can relax, enjoy the combination of fine architecture and unspoiled natural beauty, and maybe sample the local seafood, which includes rock barnacle harvested by the fishermen, at no small risk to themselves, from the rocks along the shore.

The path lies hidden among the cliffs, but **Boca do Rio** can be found between the beaches of **Burgau** and **Ingrina**, villages of whitewashed houses sloping downhill towards the sea. It was off Boca do Rio that the French ship L'Oeau sank in 1759, laden with treasure. Centuries earlier, in caves carved by the sea, the Romans built a factory where they cured seafood destined to be served as a delicacy at the Emperor's table in Rome.

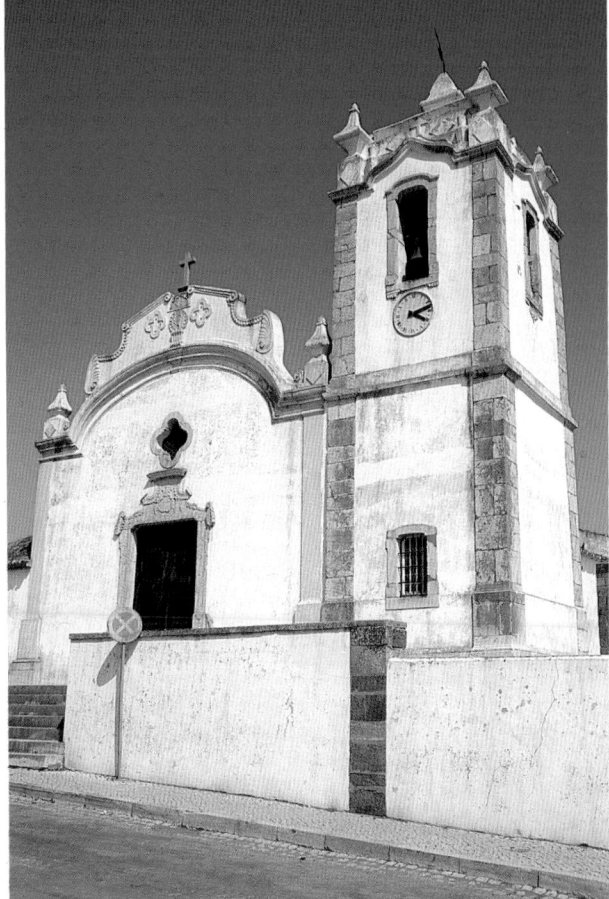

Parish Church

Dwelling in pleasing Vila do Bispo

SAGRES

The mythical promontory of **Sagres** is where the journey ends, unless we listen to our dreams. One who listened was Henry the Navigator, who decided to seek new routes over the distant horizon and chose this as the site for his school for mariners, where the saga of the Portuguese Discoveries began. Although the buildings were razed to the ground in 1587 by Sir Francis Drake on his way to a corsair attack on Lagos, the spirit of the place remained intact, guarded by the fortress formed by the bastions of Saint Anthony and Saint Barbara, dating from the XIV century. The Wind Rose set out in stone with a diameter of 43 metres guided the course of the Portuguese caravels.

Not even the great earthquake of 1755 could disturb this brooding mass of rock, at the most adding a few feet to the caverns and grottoes driven into the cliff-side by the wild sea. Although the buildings have changed radically with time, there still remain the batteries which guarded the bays of **Tonel** and **Mareta**, like sentinels and living symbols of a Land of Mariners.

The domed Chapel inside the Fort

Mariner's Compass

Fortress walls and cannon

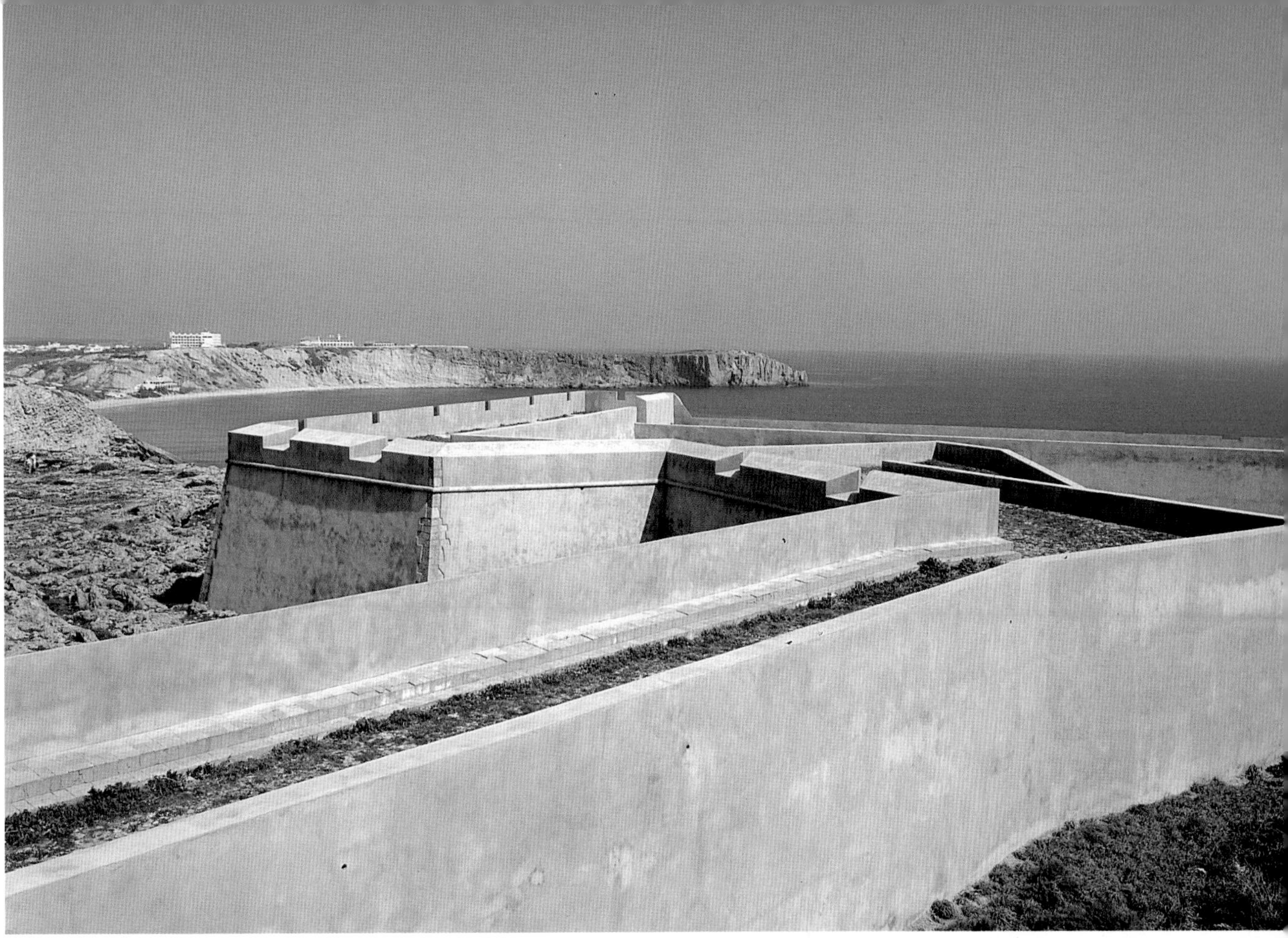

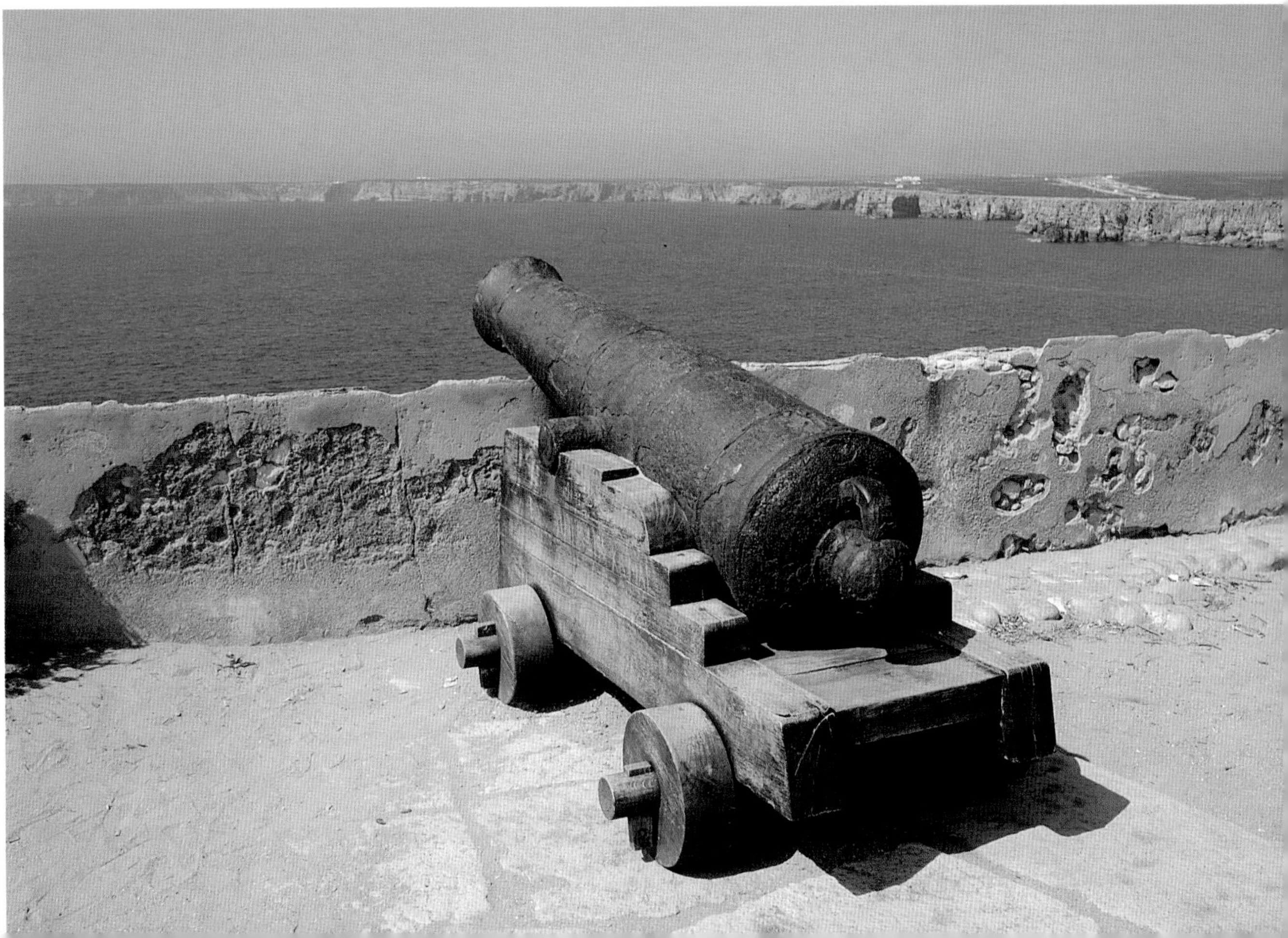

Lighthouse at Cape St. Vincent

Wall along the escarpment

The walls of the fortress at Cape St. Vincent

SÃO VICENTE

According to Christian legend, the body of St. Vicente was washed ashore beside the cape which bears his name, after his martyrdom in the fourth century. It remained there, guarded by crows, until 1173 when it was taken to Lisbon. Sacred to the Romans and possibly the site of a temple dedicated by the Greeks and Phoenicians to the gods Chronos and Melqart thousands of years ago, the **Cabo de S. Vicente** has a long association with divinity and worship.

Travelling down the west coast of Portugal, now known as the **Costa Vicentina**, the cape stands like a rampart defending the road south. A national park has been created to protect and preserve the area's natural beauty.

Cabo de S.Vicente has also seen a number of significant naval battles, and many of Europe's great naval powers have met with glory or disaster within sight of its granite rocks. In 1693 the French commander Tourville defeated a mixed squadron of British and Dutch ships here. Nearly a hundred years later, in 1780, Britain's Admiral Rodney destroyed a Spanish fleet in the same waters. Nowadays a lighthouse stands on the cape to guide ships to safe harbour. Listen to the pounding of the sea in caves along the cliff on stormy days and one can almost imagine one in hearing the bass notes of a cathedral organ.

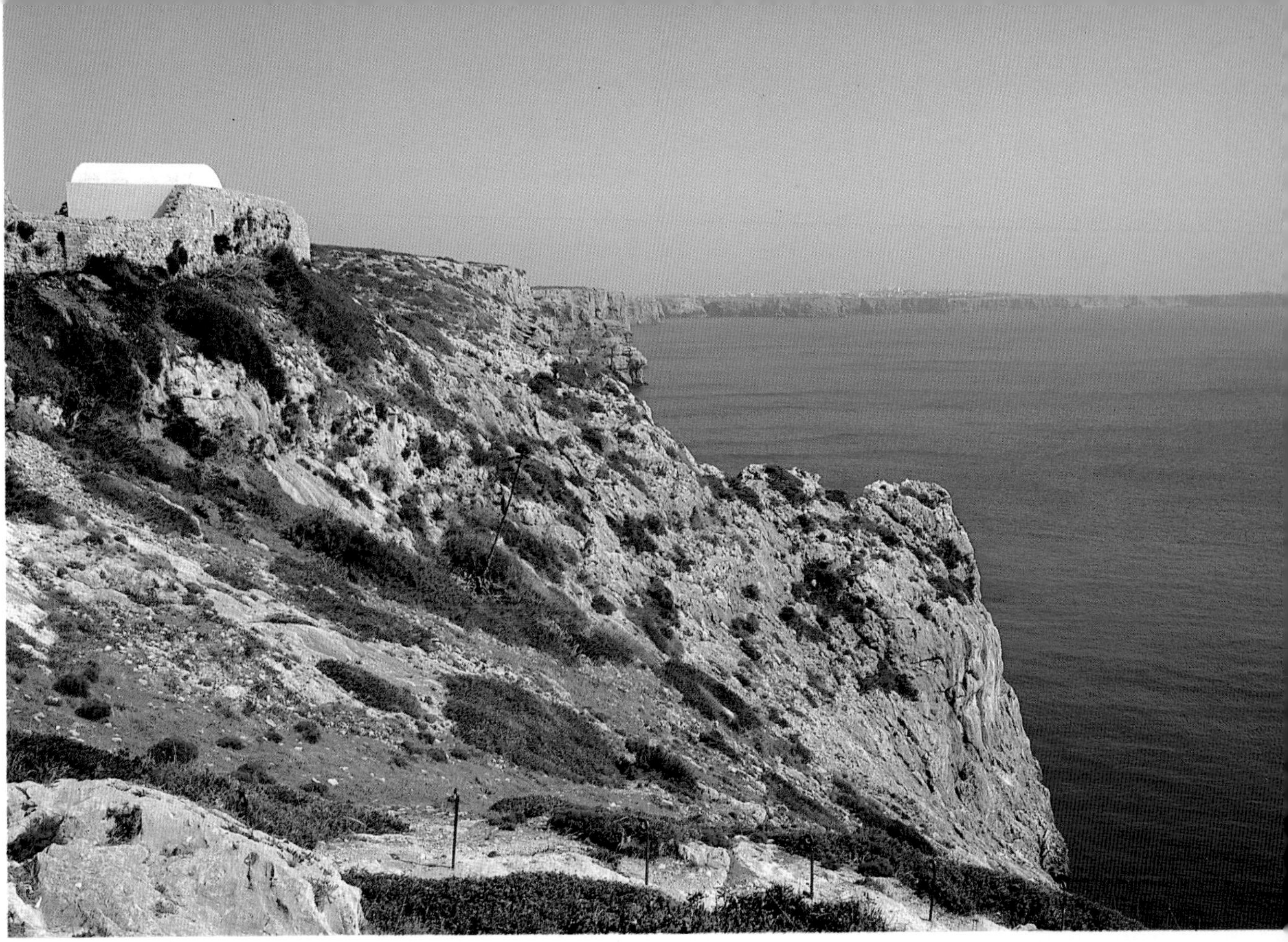

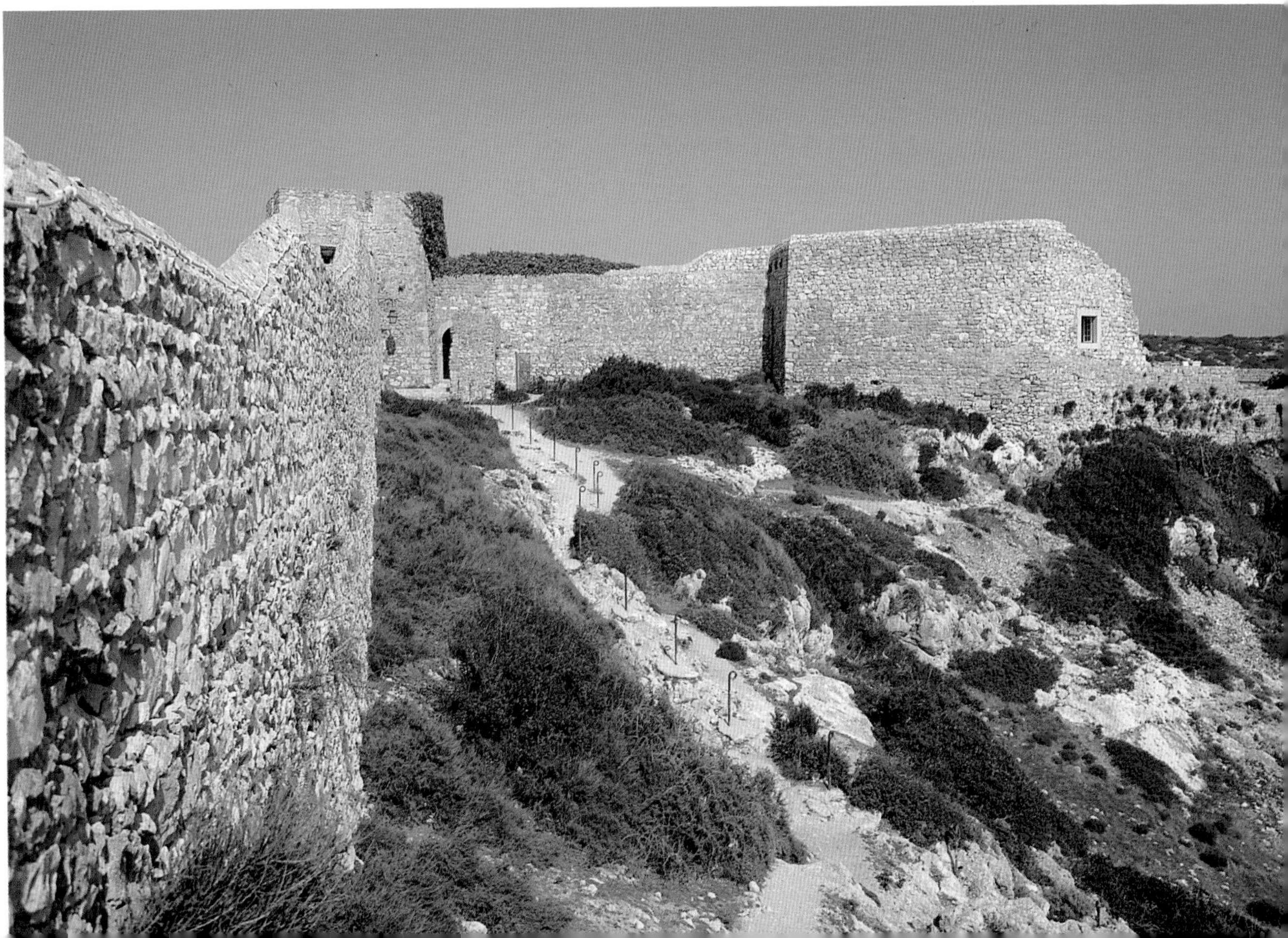

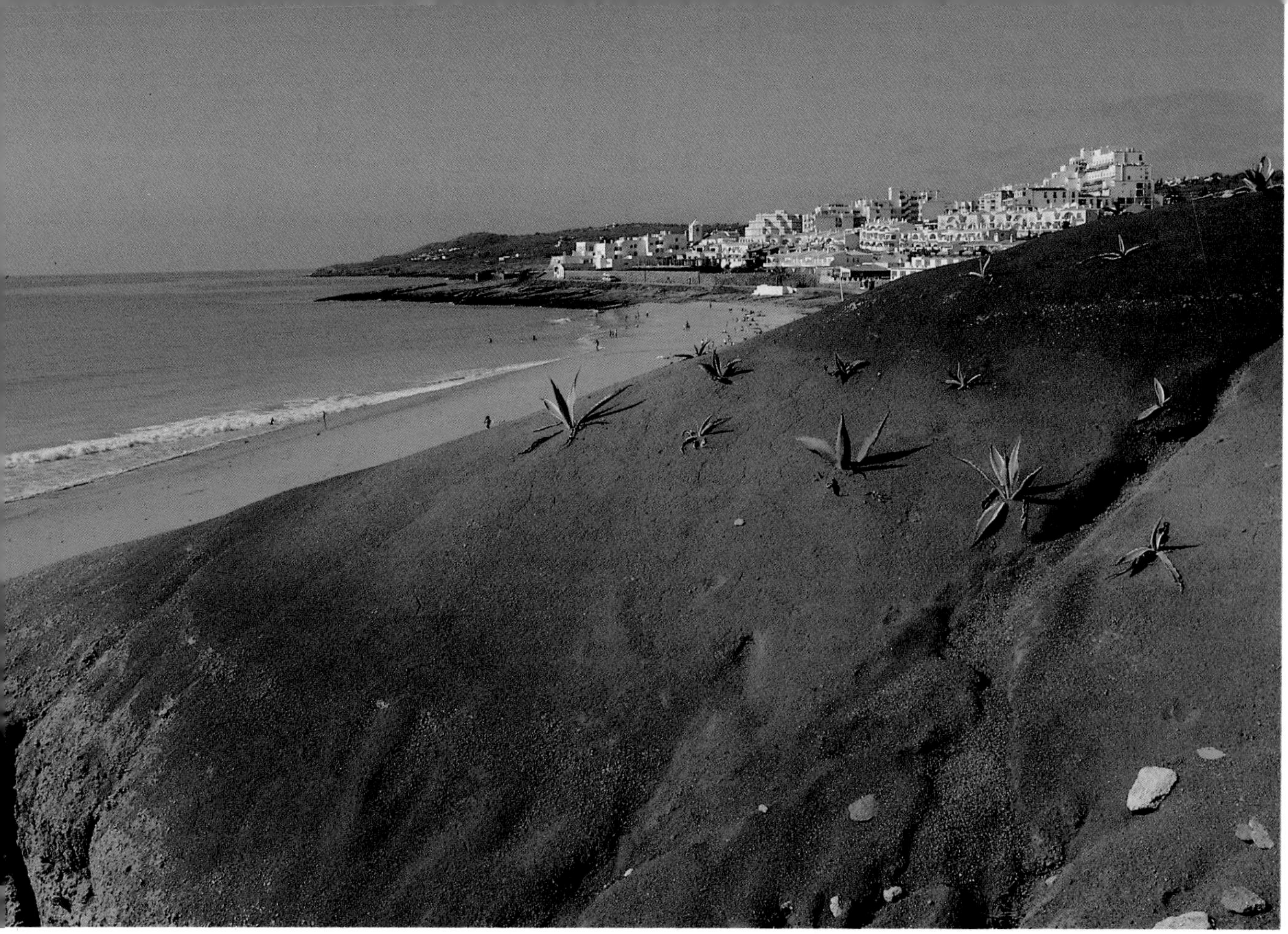

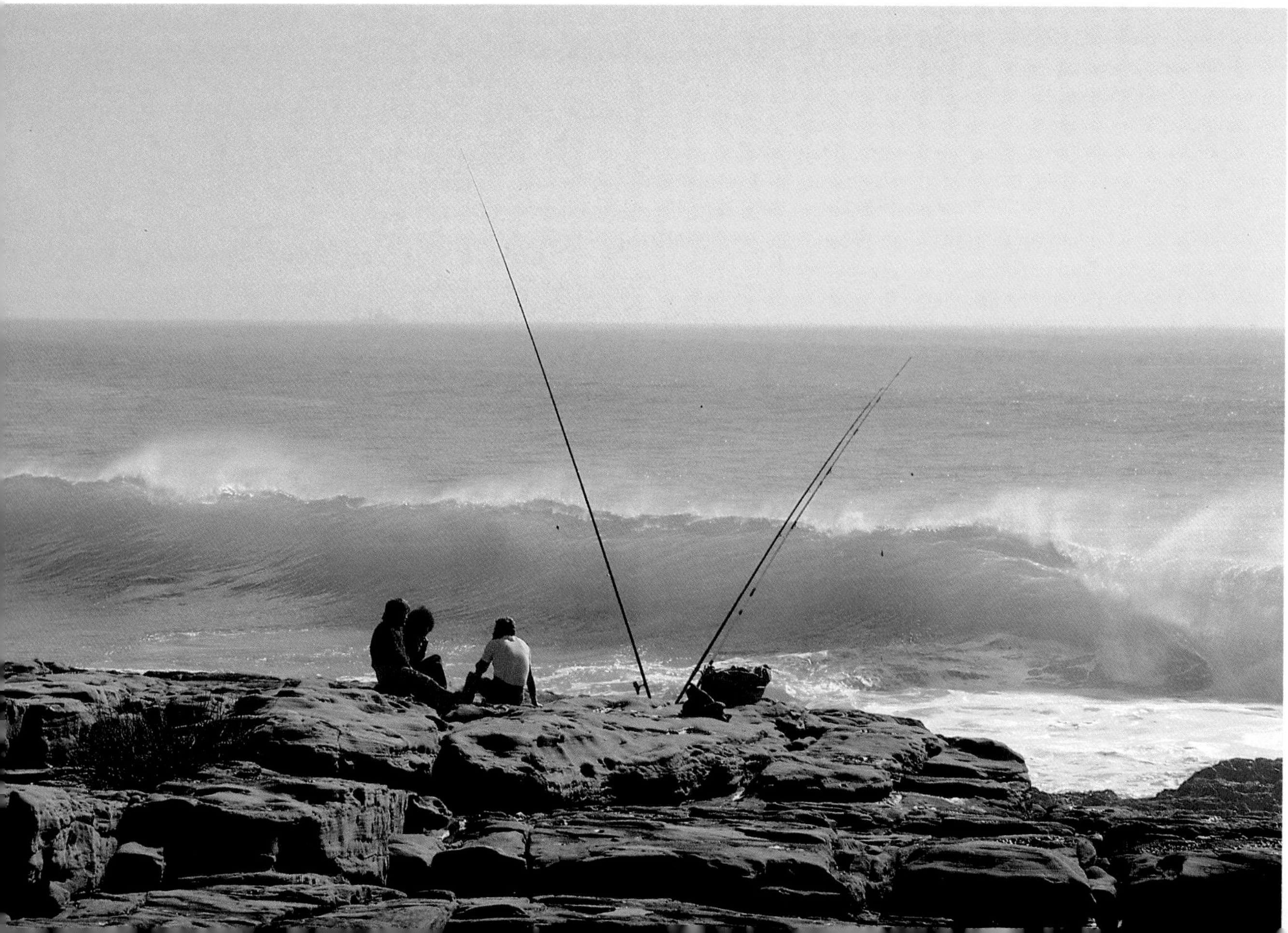

Praia da Luz

Anglers near Lagos

The picturesque town of Lagos

LAGOS

Lagos is the jewel in the Algarve crown. It has become a cosmopolitan town without selling its soul to the developers or destroying its heritage, which goes back to pre-history. Down in the bay, the white sails wave nostalgically and speak of adventures to come.

Sebastian, the boy king, set off from here for *El Ksar-el Kbir*, where he was captured, leaving Portugal to lose her independence to the Spanish.

Visitors to the city walls traditionally climb up to the Manueline window where history relates that the king attended the last open air mass before the expedition.

In the town's main square, in front of the town hall, stands the sculpture by João Cutileiro of the adolescent king, on whose shoulders weighed the cares of history. Here he is depicted as a young boy with a shy smile, pausing from play.

Up a steep flight of steps, faithfully retaining the ancient plan of the town, stands the **Church of Saint Sebastian**. On the way you can take a look at the old Slave Market, half hidden under the arcades in the **Praça da República**. As if to atone for the trade in human lives, the town boasts the extravagant baroqueries of the **Igreja de Santo António de Lagos**. The exuberant wood carvings are a lesson in the skill and imagination of the craftsmen of the time. The only point of rest is a series of paintings depicting the life of the saint attributed to Rasquinho, an eighteenth century painter from the Algarve town of Loulé.

Outside in the warm sun of *Zawaia*, the Arab name for the town they conquered in the VIII century, one of the best ways of discovering the historical centre of Lagos is to walk round the city walls, built in the XVI century on the site of previous constructions, and completely surrounding the old city. The route leads past the Governors' Palace to the **Ponta da**

13

The Castle (XIII century)

A back street of Lagos

Fort and drawbridge

Bandeira Fortress, complete with drawbridge and moat. Merchant ships have sheltered here since the times of the Phoenicians and Greeks, and the fort was built to defend the harbour from attacks by corsairs and pirates. In more peaceful times the strategic military position offers a panorama of the bay, with the sands of Meia Praia glittering in the sun. A steep climb leads up to the end of **Ponta da Piedade**, a vantage point over the fascinating rock formations and the changing colours of the sea, revealing the lie of the seabed beneath, the depths, currents and seaweed. The scene changes with every moment, with the play of sea, rock and light.

The tiny beaches tucked into the cliffs can be reached by a steep climb down or by boat, through arches and other rock formations, each given its own colourful name by the local fishermen.

The inhabitants of Lagos speak in sweet, lilting tones. Hearing them tell a story, or even giving the time of day, is like listening to a melody, in which

each phrase grows in a crescendo to a sharp climax, where the vowels fade into nothing.

The local pastries and marzipan sweets are second to none: miniature fruits and animals in bright colours and subtly varying flavours.

Lagos is fortunate in its beaches. A freak of the winds has spared the town the Atlantic breakers which crash against the Sagres cliffs only a few miles to the west. Instead, the climate is gentle and the sea welcoming.

But Lagos is a modern city. Rather than resting on the laurels of millennia, it has kept up with the times, and shopping here is like in any other European capital.

Lagos offers easy sophistication and an effortless balance between local traditions, historic greatness and modern reality: this is a city at peace with itself.

Igreja de Santo António (XVIII century)

THE LAGOS MUSEUM

The **Municipal Museum** of Lagos avoids the musty smell of antiquity ranged in glass cases. Instead, the museum seeks to bring to life the arts and crafts of the men and women who made the history of the town and its monuments and the tools of their trades. The archeological section displays finds from the stone age to the Roman occupation. A large part of this is rightly given over to the Iberian period, as Lagos played host to one of the pioneers of a sense of Portuguese nationality, Sertorius, companion in arms to Viriatus, regarded as the first man to have dreamed of building a single nation.

The museum has an excellent folk history section, with a display of farming tools, fishing tackle and regional crafts, including outstanding examples of bobbin lace, basket work and pottery. Located next door to the Igreja de Santo António de Lagos, the Museum proudly displays the Charter granted by King Manuel and the sixteenth century diptych representing the Annunciation and the Presentation at the Temple. The museum is one of the best reasons for visiting Lagos.

Azulejos panels at the entrance hall

Fragments of Roman artifacts

Ethnography of the Algarve

Nossa Senhora do Livramento (terracotta)

Marble sculpture of Nossa Senhora da Conceição

Rock formations at Praia Dona Ana

PRAIA DONA ANA

To appreciate the contrast between the gentle countryside and the cosmopolitan bustle of Lagos, take the winding road leading to **Praia Dona Ana**. Twisted fig trees, locust trees bent with age and beside them the thin and delicate almond trees. Tiny gardens bristle with life. And suddenly, almost when you least expect it, you arrive at the cliffs and the sea stretches beneath you.

This is not the only surprise. Until you come in sight of the beach the landscape seems undecided, hesitating between land and sea. Finally the beach appears, a small curve of sand fringed by ochre cliffs, where the rocks, washed and worn by the sea, are constantly changing.

From here, the horizon on one side is dominated by warm waters dotted with rocks which alter in colour with the changing hues of the sunlight, and on the other side by the almost sheer rise of the cliffs. Down by the breakwater pools of crystal clear water and tiny grottos where the hum of the sea weaves strange melodies.

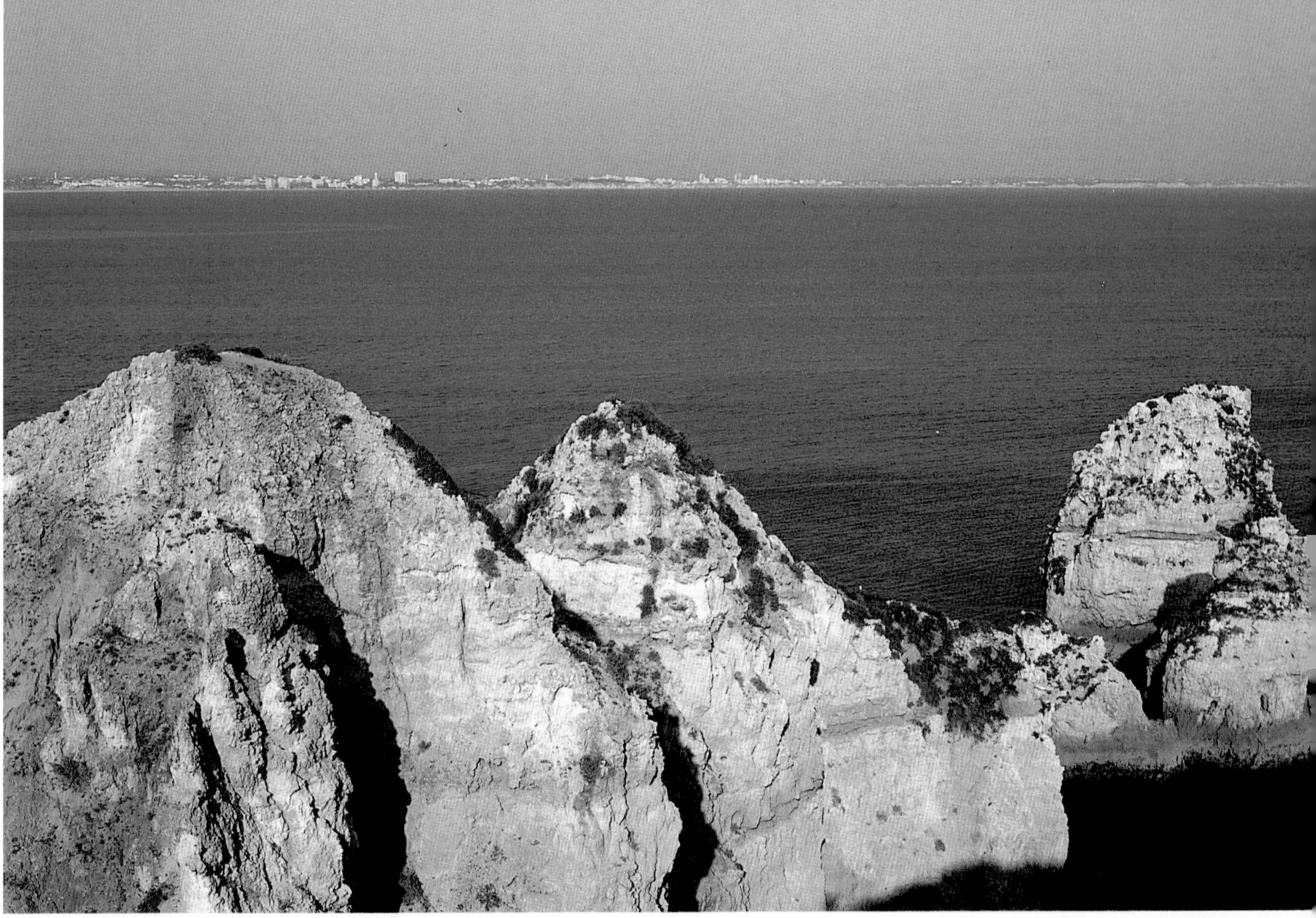

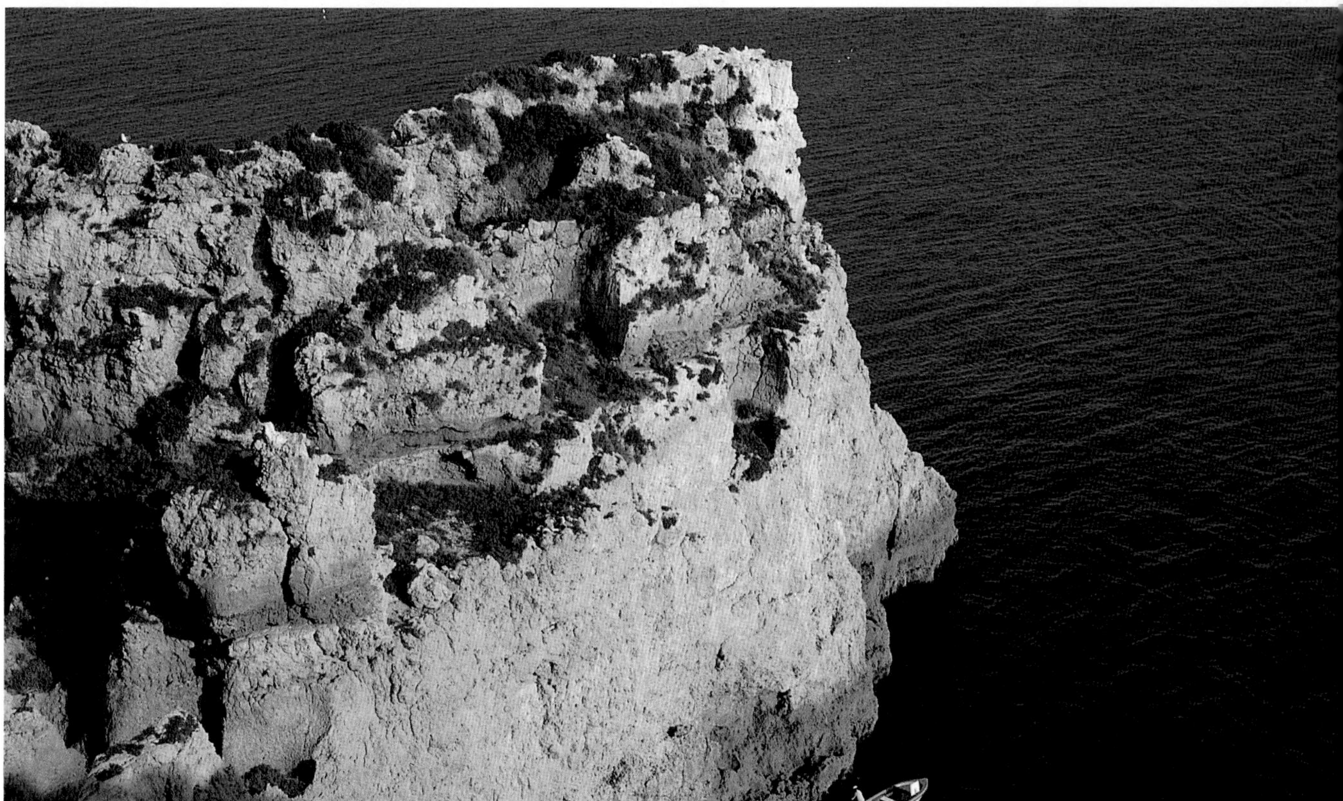

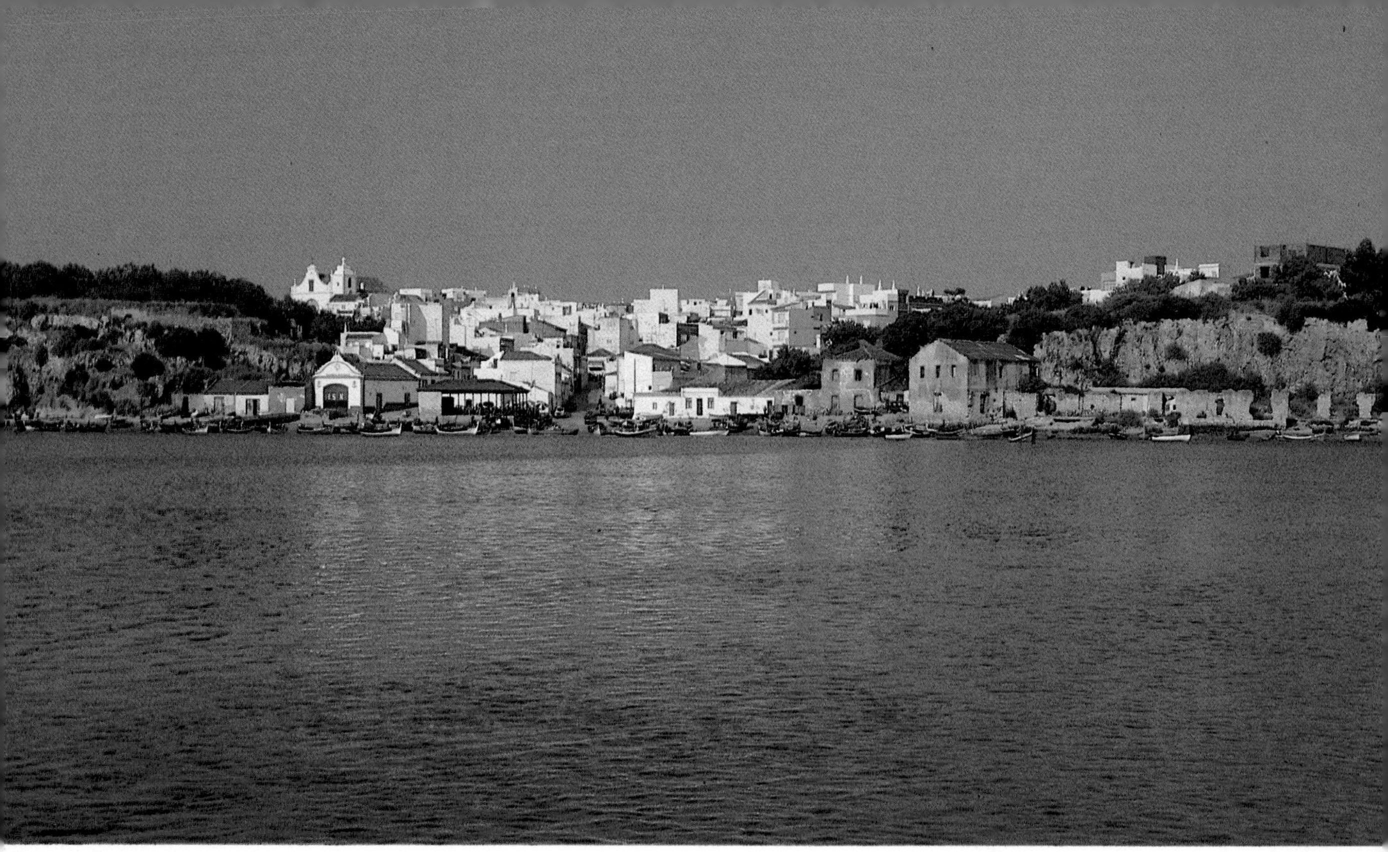

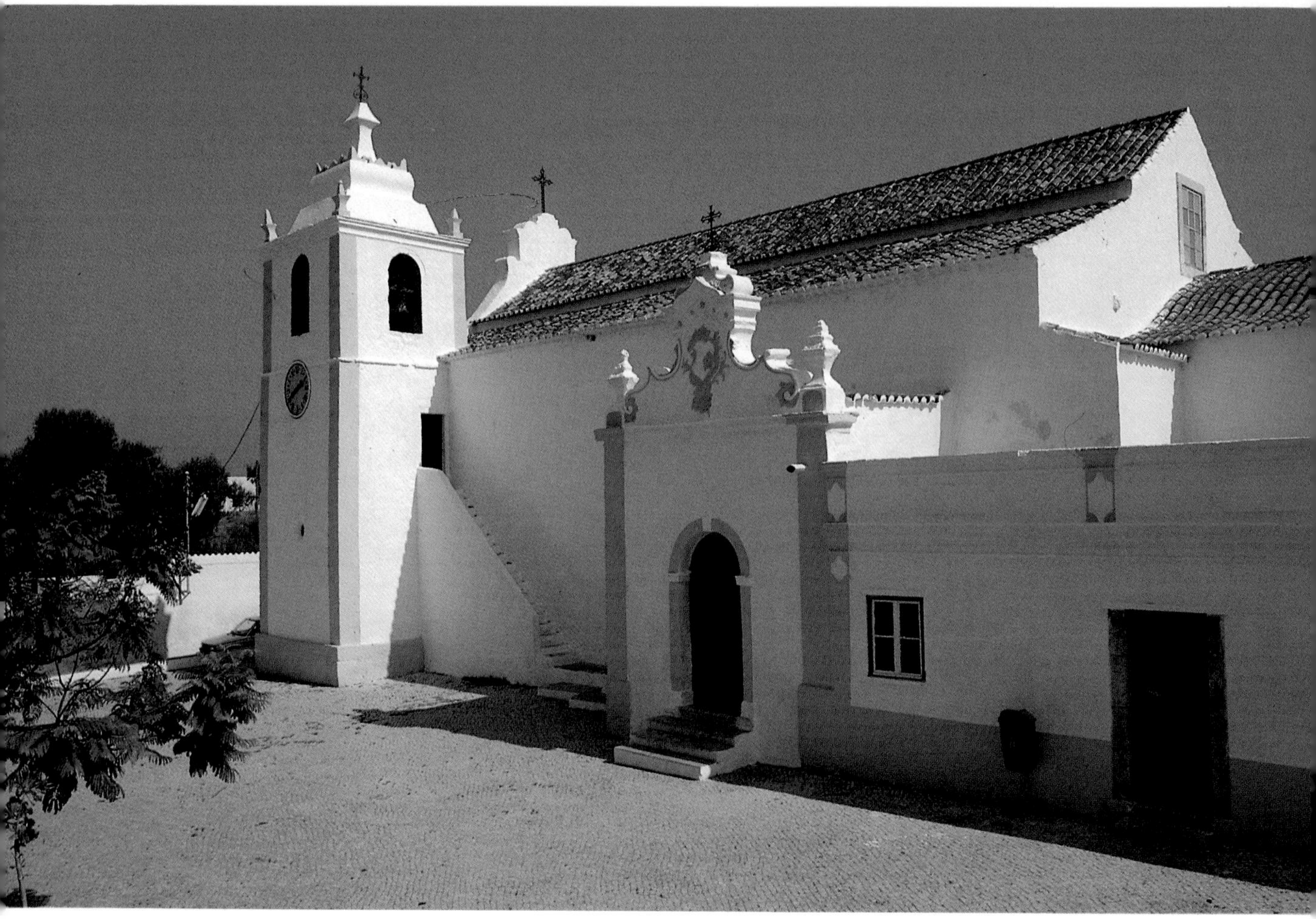

View of Alvor

The XVI Century Parish Church of Alvor

Fishing boats in the Portimão harbour

ALVOR

Alvor is a village on the water and surrounded by water. Living on a river mouth with islands and lagoons, the local fishermen work the channels and pools like water gardens, catching clams. This is a centuries old occupation, as old as the **Manueline portico** on the parish church and its interior of red sandstone and eighteenth century tiles.

Alvor is also a stopover for migratory birds. On their long journey south from the north of Europe, great flocks descend each year on the dunes.

PORTIMÃO

The soul of Portimão is still to be found on the waterfront, where in days gone by only small traditional fishing craft would dock, bringing back their trawl of sardines. Factories grew up around the port, and men moved in to work in them. When the sardine boats come in, the fish is unloaded in small baskets passed in a gentle rhythm from the deck to the quay, a daily ritual. Just over the way, little restaurants spread their tables outside and serve up the sea-fresh sardines with thick slices of home made bread, the local light wine and a salad of local produce. Starting in the thirties, Portimão was rediscovered as a holiday resort, gaining a reputation among English intellectuals, attracted by the exotic beauty of **Praia da Rocha**. The town has never looked back, and the port and the surrounding area are now an all year round holiday centre.

The earthquake of 1755 destroyed nearly all traces of the past. All that remains are the ancient burial

View of the Portimão harbour

The Village of Ferragudo and its XVI century castle

ground at **Alcalar**, dating from 1600 BC, and **Abicada**, a IV century Roman villa. The **Parish Church**, rebuilt after the catastrophe, retains a doorway from the old building, with unusual carvings depicting men and women ready for battle, with no distinction in regard to dress or arms. The way in and out of Portimão is over the Ribeira do Arade, where the old iron bridge has recently been joined by an elegant modern structure in concrete. It is worth the traveller's time to take the winding turn-off to **Estombar**, if only to see the **Parish Church** which stands like an imposing cathedral in proportion to the village square. Inside, there are magnificent tiles from the eighteenth century and a small masterpiece of XVI century colonnades, sculpted in red sandstone with a wealth of details.

FERRAGUDO

The Fortress of Saint John was built in Ferragudo to guard the mouth of the river Arade, the line of communication between Portimão and Silves. This was in the turbulent days of the XVI century when Spanish, Dutch and English fleets attacked the coast in the struggle for the colonial dominions. Today Ferragudo is a leisurely holiday retreat, where pleasure boats leave to sail up the Arade, following the course of the Roman, Arab and Norse vessels which journeyed up to Silves, passing by the **Hermitage of Nossa Senhora do Rosário** which stands on an island in the river, through a landscape where cliffs, hills and grottos roll down to the river bank.

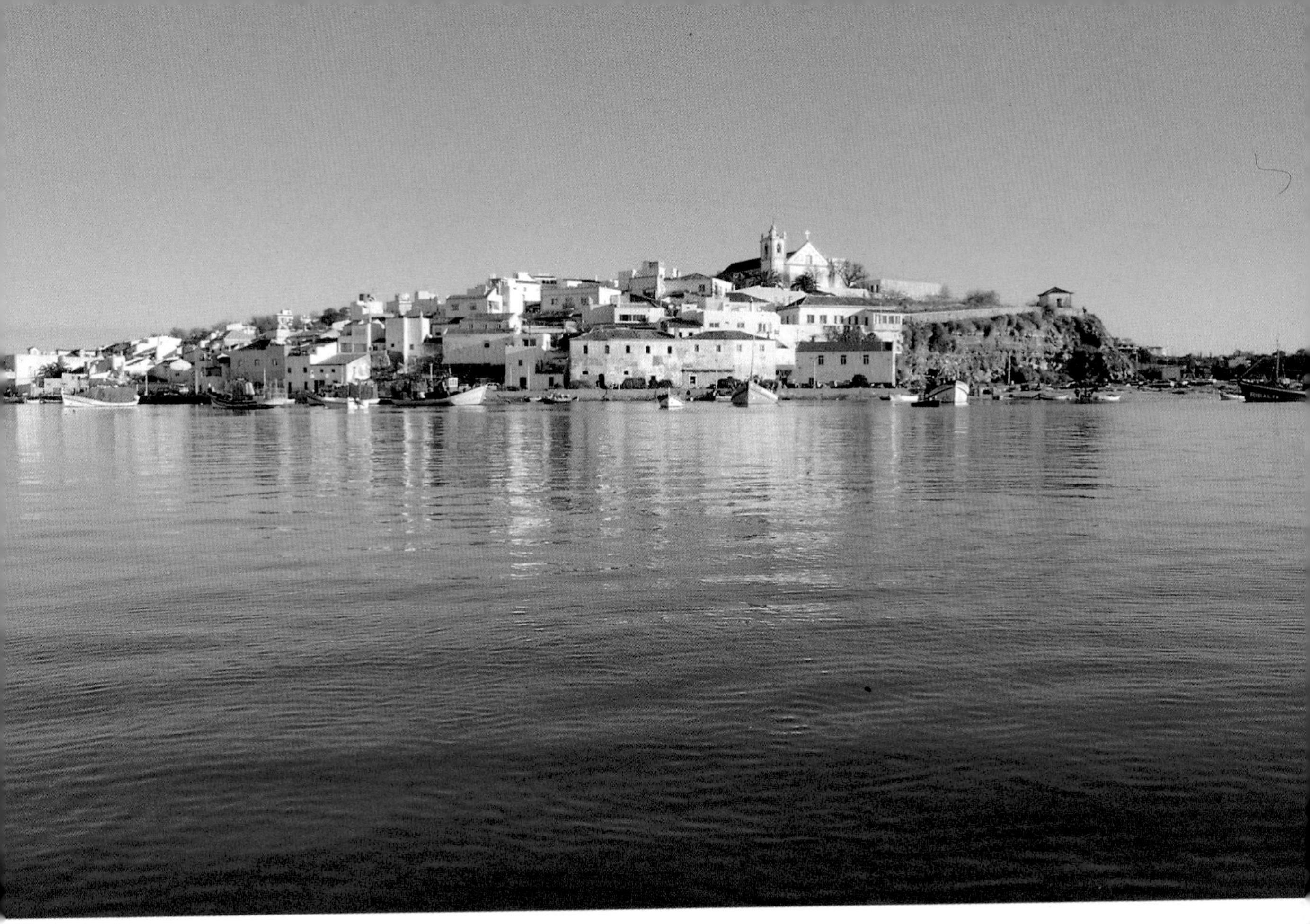

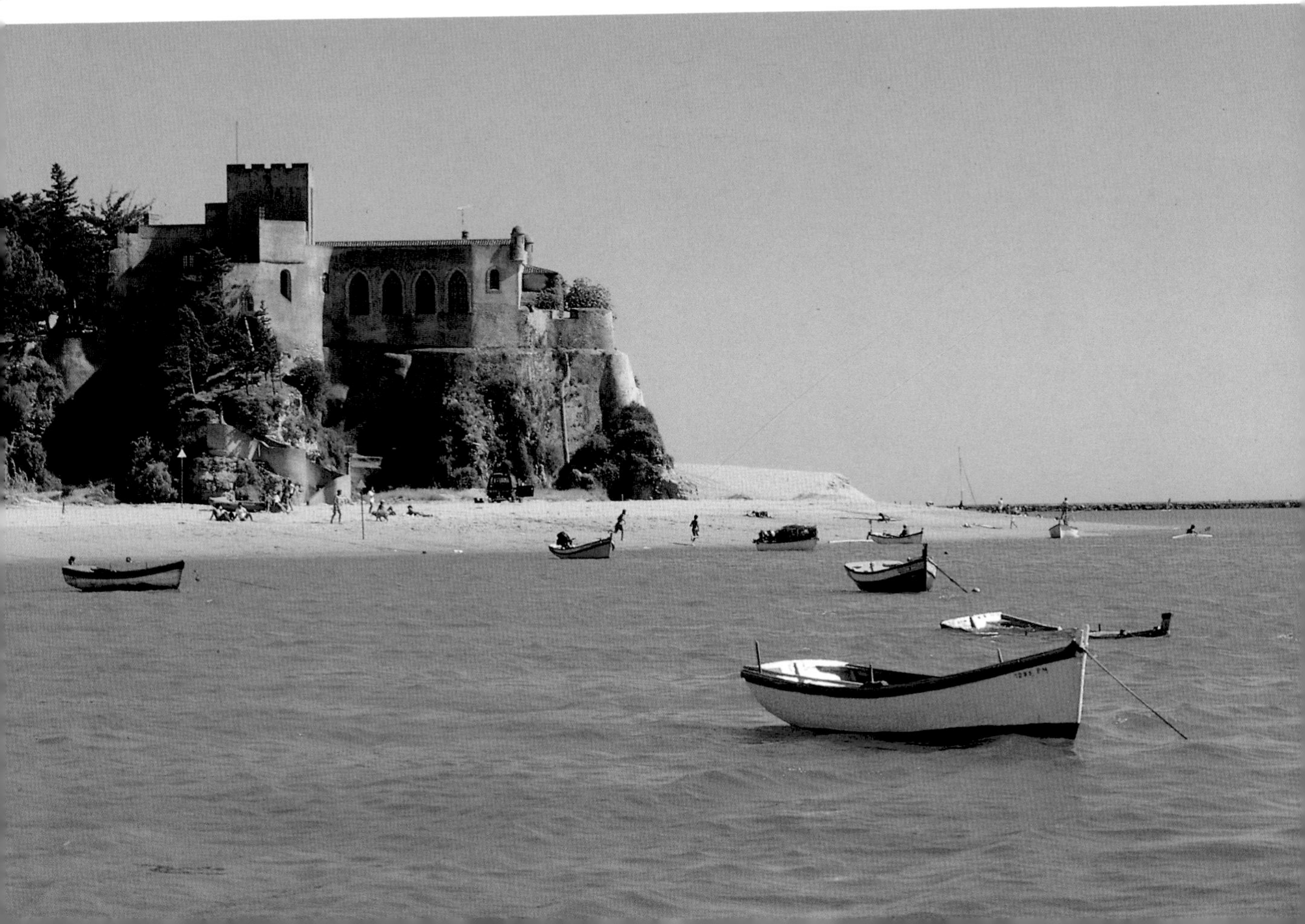

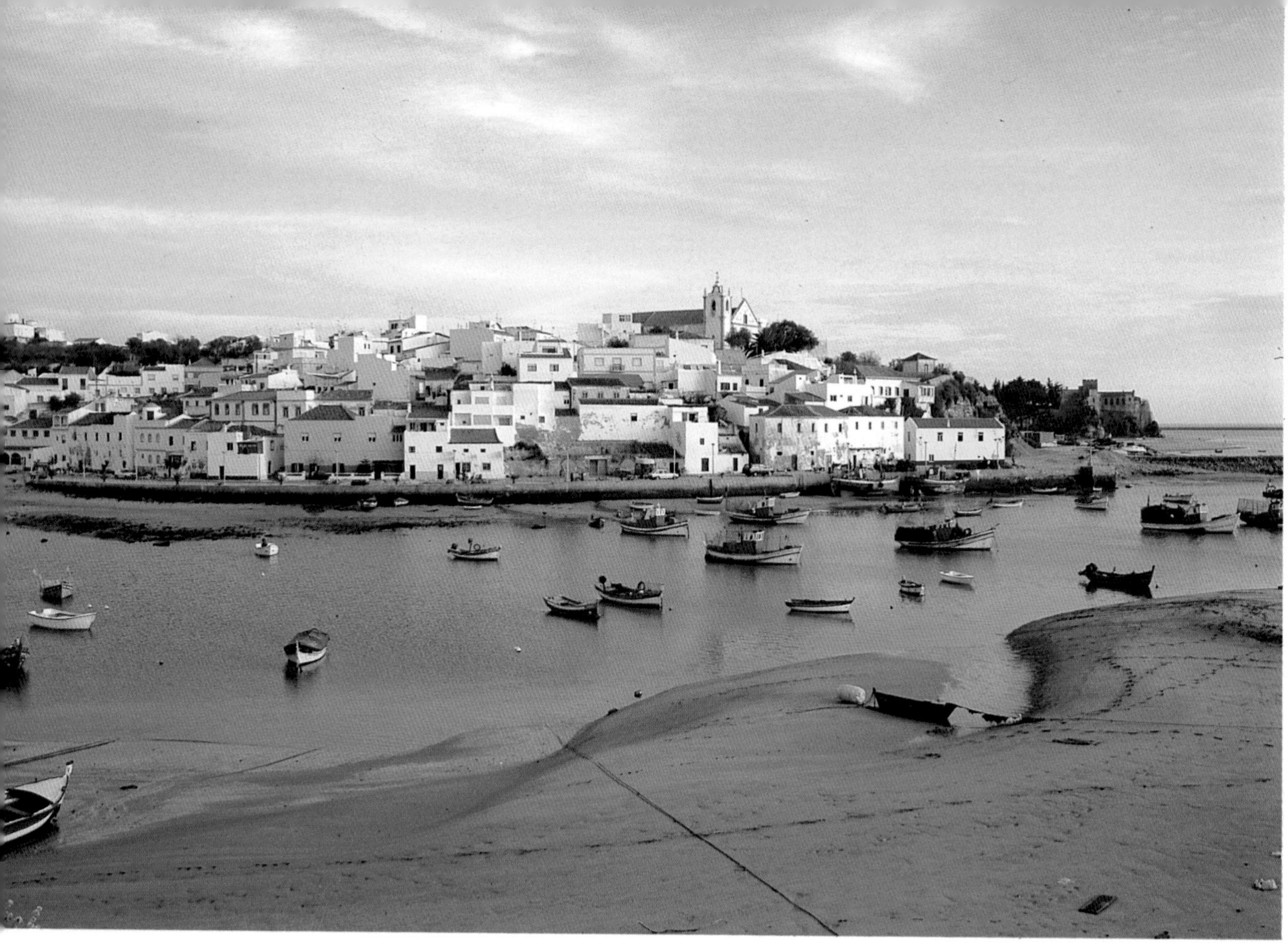

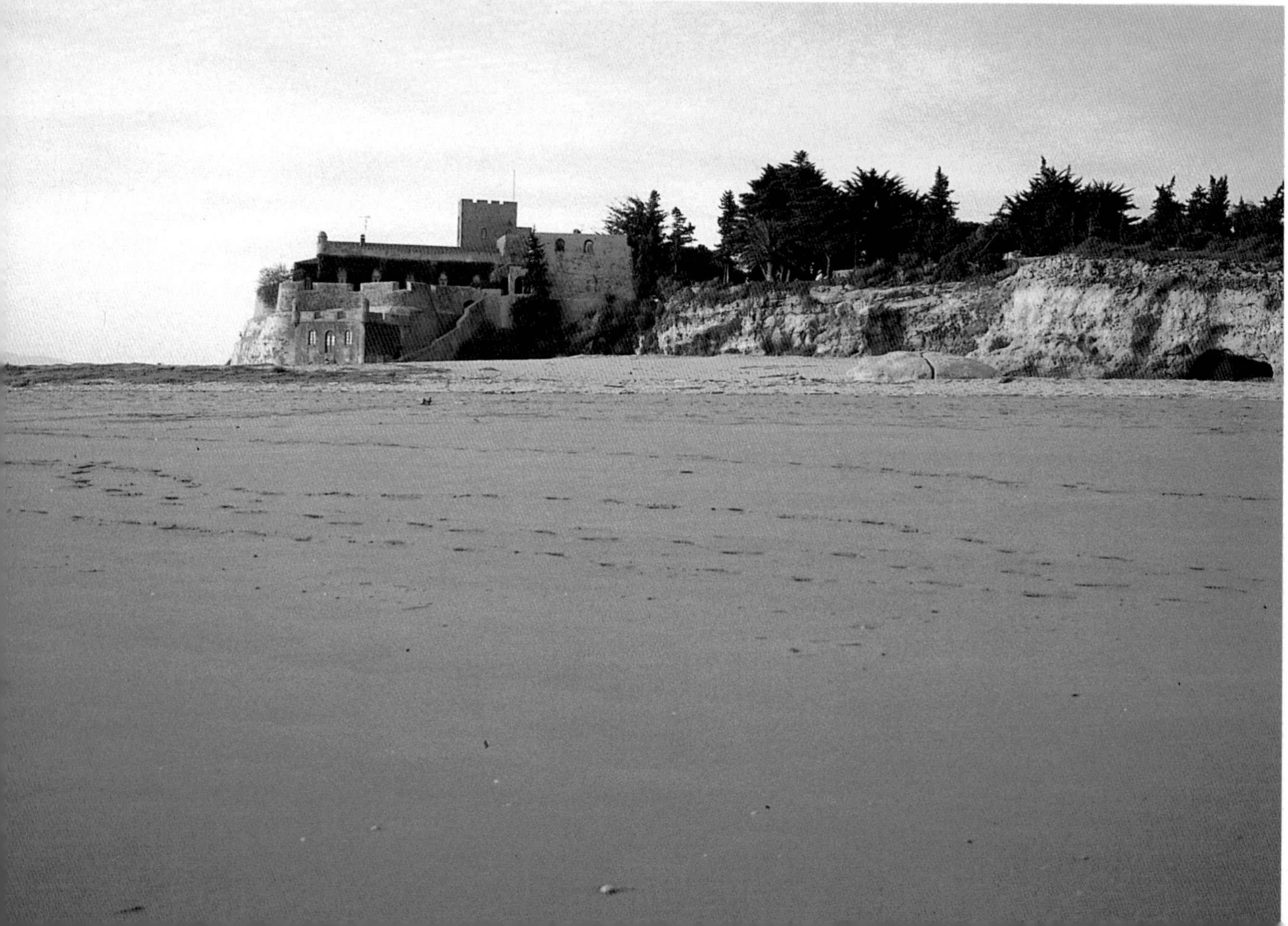

Praia da Rocha

Views of Ferragudo and Castle

PRAIA DA ROCHA

The sand stretches into the distance as far as the eye can see, bathed in golden sunlight, fringed by the gentle white breakwater, as far as the rocks which rise up like ancient monuments. The soft sand nestles against the hard rock, and the bright sea flickers beneath the blood red cliffs, worn away by wind and tide. Like a sculptor wielding the chisel of time, nature has moulded **Praia da Rocha**, capturing the soul of the Algarve.

MONCHIQUE

The green mountains of the **Serra de Monchique** form a green barrier between the Algarve and the Alentejo. The hills rise up suddenly, sheltering hidden valleys and deep ravines, the slopes wooded with chestnut, cork oaks and pine, giving way to clearings ablaze with flowers: daisies, oleander and rosemary. Viewed from **Alto da Fóia** (902 m), the hills range below like a grassy green carpet, and in the distance the sea glitters along the coast. The village hugs the rugged hillside, and the houses tumble down to the square fronted by the **Parish Church** with its exuberant Manueline doorway.

Caldas de Monchique is a spa where the thermal waters were tapped by both Romans and Arabs. Hidden in narrow mountain ravine, the spa operates to this day.

Monchique is an invitation to calm, where the springs well up from the hillside, and the chill waters play in the warm sunshine.

The view from Mount Fóia

Hidden away in a green valley is the spa of Caldas de Monchique on the east side of Mount Fóia

General view of the city

SILVES

Silves has preserved its Arab past more clearly than any other town in the Algarve. Capital of the Algarve for centuries, Silves was a city of luxury, where sages and poets held court, and merchants traded with the Mediterranean. When relations with North Africa were broken off and the River Arade slowly silted up, the city's influence paled, giving way to Lagos.

The fortress is a complex of defensive towers and a bastion, linked by high walls. The Arabs built the castle on the site of previous Phoenicians and Roman constructions. The red stone, like red clay, paradoxically makes the castle look as if it has just been finished. The Cistern of the *Moura Encantada* (enchanted mooress), the **Arco da Rebola** and the remains of the palace of Aben Afan, the last Arabic king, are reminders of other lives and cultures.

The **Cathedral**, seven centuries old, was built on the site of the mosque on the orders of Afonso X, the Wise, who was king of Castille and by feudal rights lorded over the Algarve in the XIII century. This Gothic cathedral was the centre of the Algarve diocese until the XVI century. Another church, that of Our Lady of the Martyrs, guards the tombs of crusaders who lost their lives when the city was first taken.The way to the coast over the Arade is still over the medieval bridge, built to replace the old Roman bridge. The visitor can take the road as far as Rocha Branca, a Greek trading post, and then go up to **Monte da Jóia** for the views, with the castle silhouetted against the horizon, surrounded by the bright green of orange, almond and lotus groves.

The Moorish Cistern at the Silves Museum

The statue of King Sancho I who conquered Silves to the Moors in 1189

The Moorish Castle with its imposing walls and courtyard

THE SILVES MUSEUM

The older inhabitants of the town used to call it "the hole" until archeologists discovered that it was a cistern, built by the Moors in the XI century.

As the excavations progressed a red sandstone cistern more than 10 metres high came to light. Three vaulted niches open onto the central well, and a stairway covered in semi-circular vaulting winds round the whole structure. The cistern has been restored and the present **Museum of Silves** built around it. The interaction between the historical remains of the past and the architecture of today yields a fascinating commentary on modern conceptions of space and design. The museum and its buildings are a true work of art, and contain an important collection of Moorish artefacts from the region. These include ceramics, iron goods and a delicately worked pin made from bone, and other pieces of great artistic value.

CARVOEIRO

By a trick of the tides, the small inlet of Carvoeiro is protected between high cliffs. The cove offers shelter to traditional fishing boats, decorated with bright naive paintings. Cliffs of ochre stone, worn into tracery, line the turquoise sea as far as the **Cape.** On the way stands the hermitage, the work of man, whilst the strange vaulted grotto of **Algar Seco** echoes like a cathedral carved by the wind and the sea.

ALCANTARILHA

The houses of Alcantarilha gaze over the green of the vineyards and orange groves stretching down to the sea, whose blue blurs with the horizon. The locals are proud of their **Capela dos Ossos** (the bone-lined chapel), which can be visited in the Manueline parish church. A fine XVI century portico marks the entry to the **Capela da Misericórdia.**
Along a quiet country path towards Algoz a prehistoric menhir stands three metres tall; known as the Penedo Grande, it serves as a reminder of the ancient peoples who once lived here.

Jacarandas on a street in Silves

Beach and town of Carvoeiro

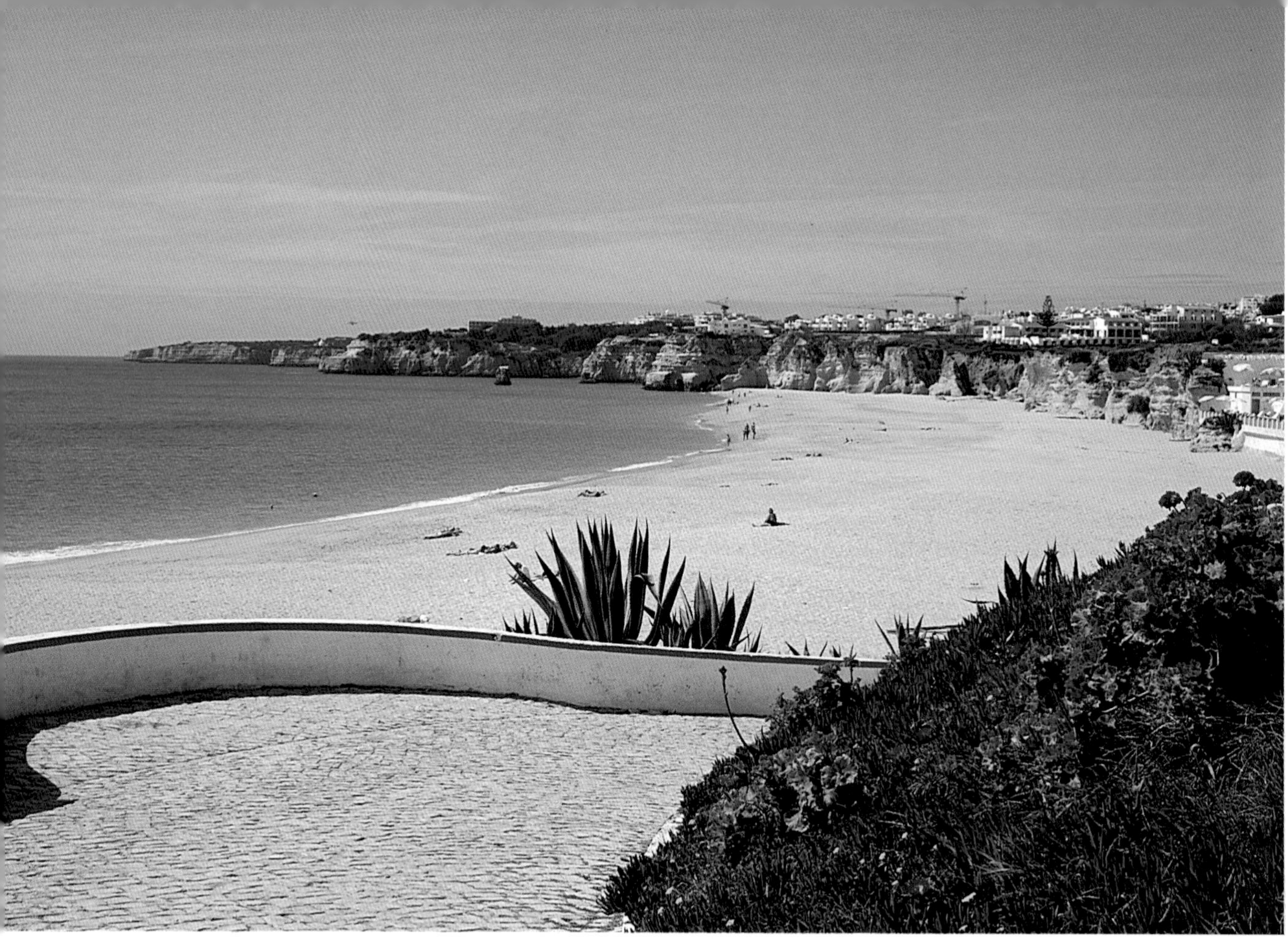

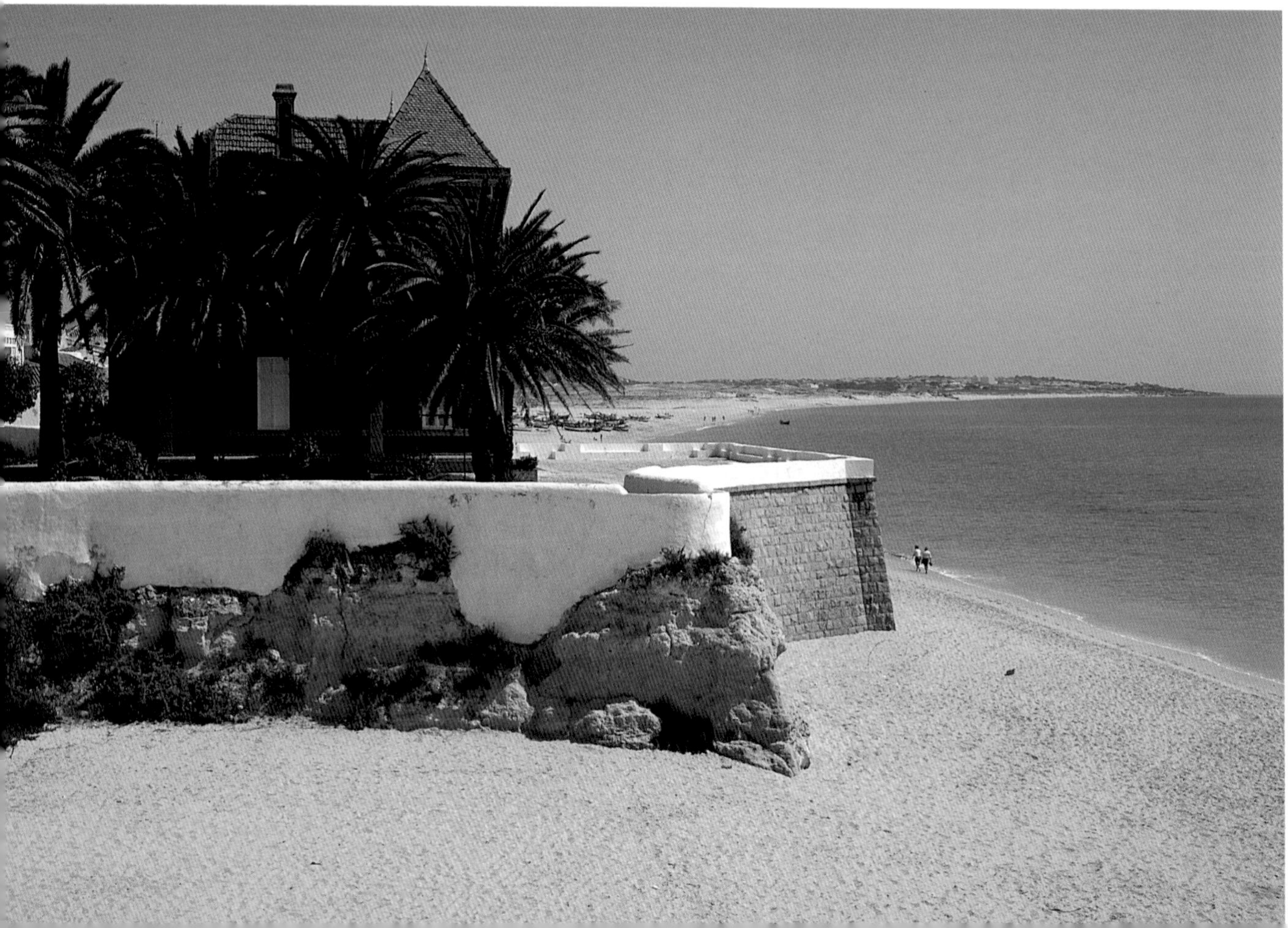

ARMAÇÃO DE PÊRA

The origins of the name Armação de Pêra have been lost over the centuries. The fishermen built and anchored their boats at the beach of modern-day **Armação,** returning at night to the village of **Pêra,** a few kilometres inland. The village has retained its traditional character, and the **Parish Church** boasts ornate rococo carving around the high altar. The **Igreja de S. Francisco**, despite damage in the earthquake, still displays paintings in the choir and the nave.

Craftsmen have kept alive local skills of *empreita,* articles hand woven from palm leaves, and colourful ceramics. The seafront has evolved into a sophisticated holiday resort, with a long inviting beach. Small fishing craft are now to be seen alongside the bright sails of windsurfers. When the tide makes fishing impossible, fishermen will hire their boats and services to visitors who want to see the grotto at Pontal, taking them along the rugged coast where the sea washes through eccentric rock formations.

The beach at Armação de Pêra

Fishing boats

Following pages:
Fishing boats at Armação de Pêra;
rocky Algarve near Albufeira

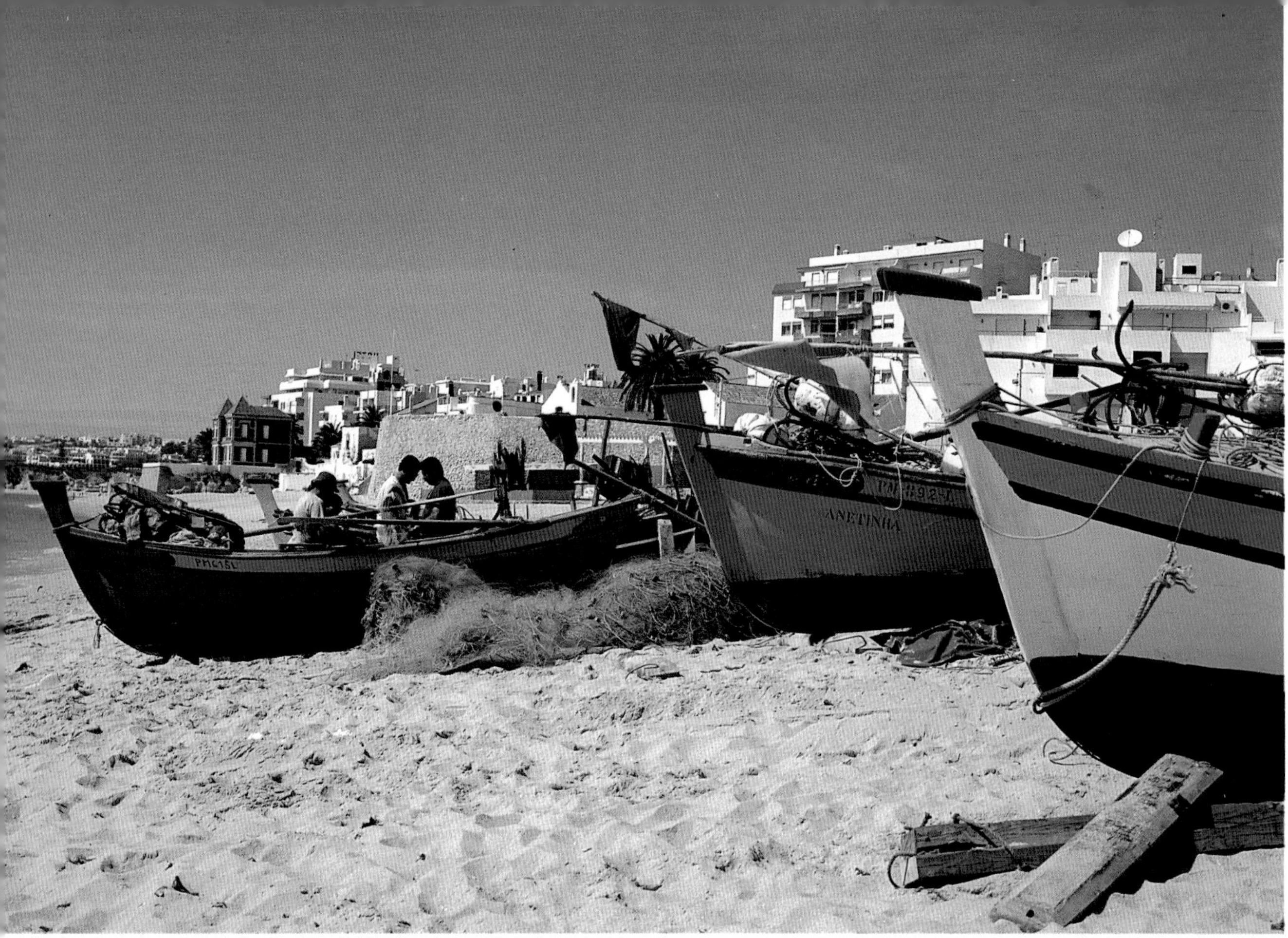
ANETINHA

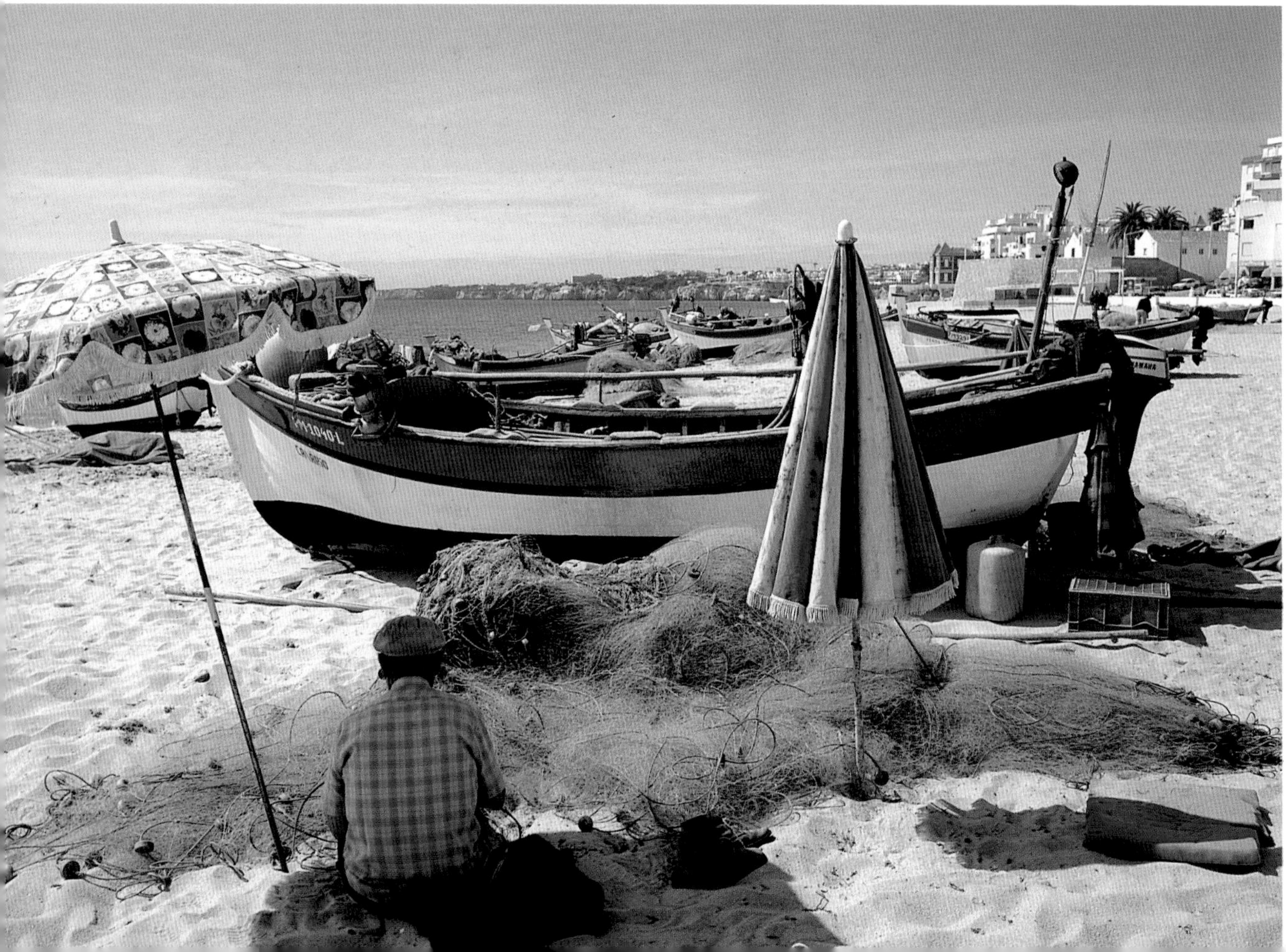

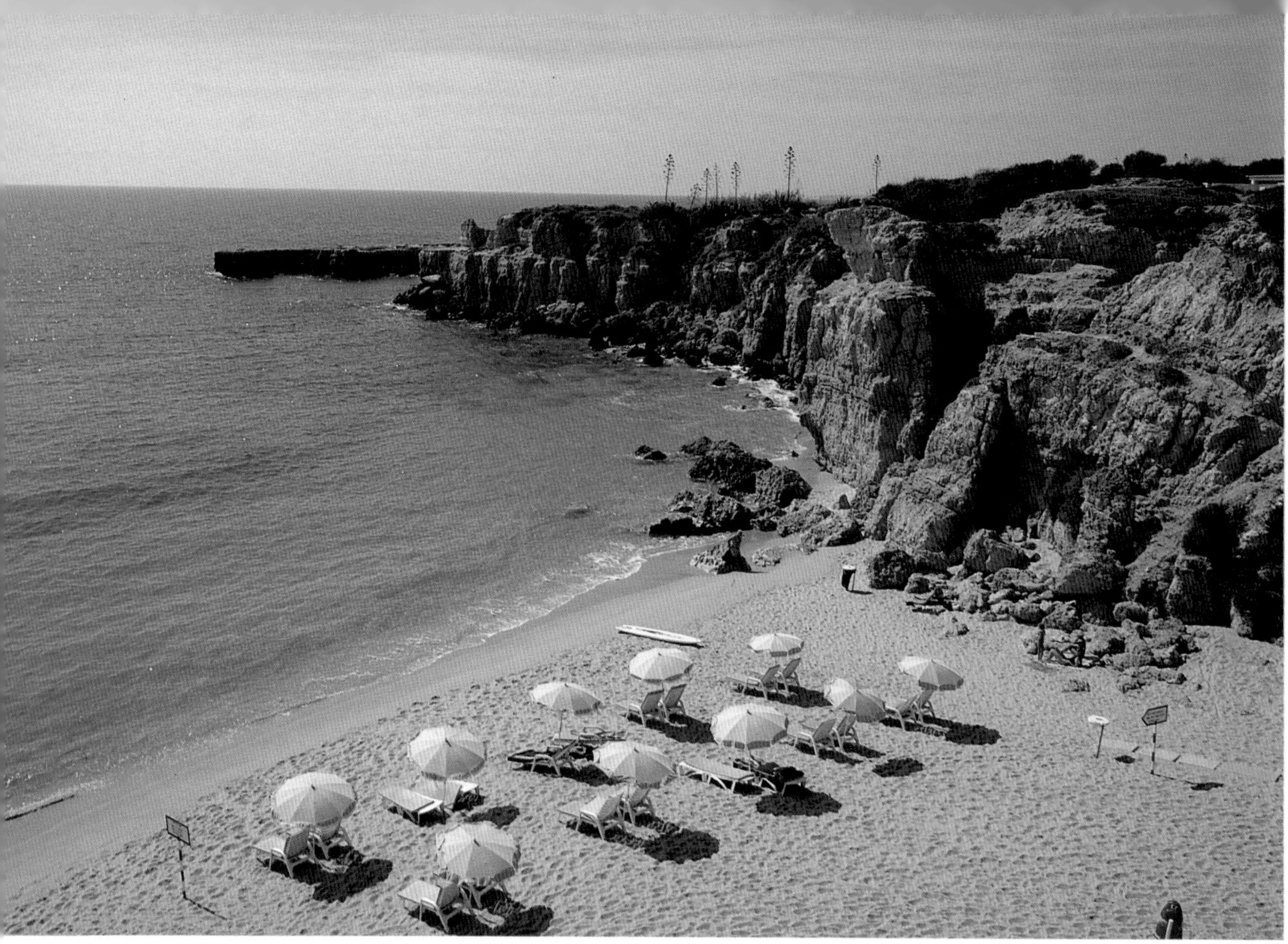

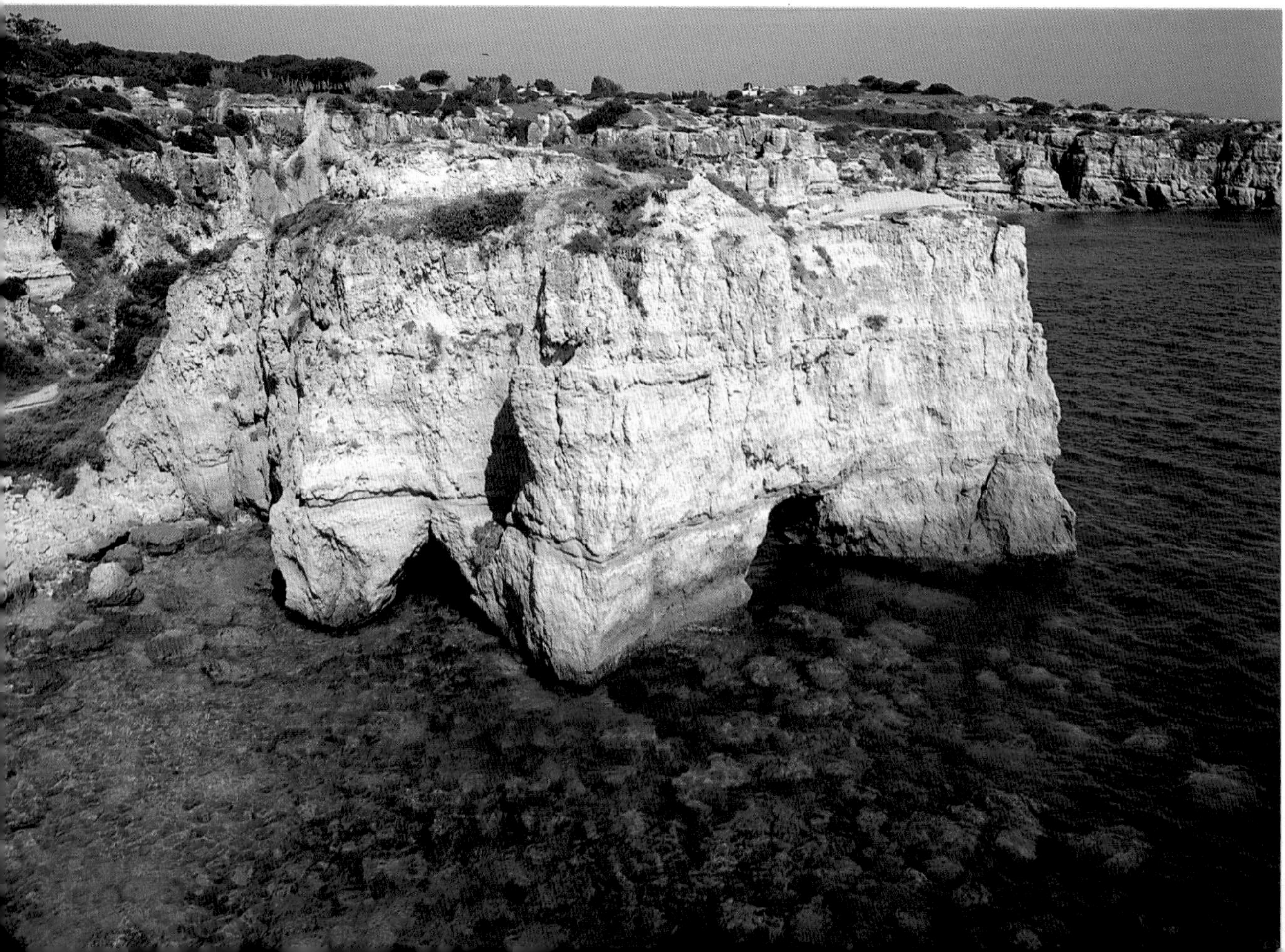

A cove in the rocks and
typical rock formations on the Algarve
coast

The coast near Baleeira and a
secluded beach near Albufeira

Following pages:
strange rock formation near Baleeira
and a crevice on the cliff

ALBUFEIRA

The Arabs rightly named Albufeira Castle of the Sea, *Al-Bhuera*, whilst centuries before the Romans called it *Ballum*. The end of the trade with Morocco all but ruined this centuries-old fishing port. But the fishermen and merchants rebuilt their town and fortifications, and when it was visited in the XVI Century by the king, Sebastian the Desired, it boasted a fort and walls of defence against the English and French corsairs, then the scourge of the Algarve coast.

Still retaining the character of a fishing village, Albufeira is today renowned as a lively pleasure resort. The winding streets of the old town lead to the Praça da República, the cosmopolitan centre. Nearby stands the **Capela da Misericórdia**, a XVI century chapel on the site of an Arabic Mosque; this is a Manueline construction with ribbed vaulting. The steep alleyways lead inevitably to the beach where the boats are laid up and the fishermen ply their lively trade. The harbour walls offer a panorama of the white houses tumbling down the cliff to the sea.

Igreja Matriz

Fishermen's Beach

General view of Albufeira

The Old Town

RESTAURANTE
O TUNEL
Coca-Cola
BAR
BEER SHOP
O TUNEL
RESTAURANTE
TURISMO

Fishermen's Beach

Striking rock formation on the beach

Warm seas and golden sands typify
the coastal attraction of the Algarve

The Marina at Vilamoura

Holiday apartments

A first-class hotel in Vilamoura

VILAMOURA

Vilamoura stands as a monument to the years since the 60's which have seen the Algarve become an international focus for recreation and leisure activities. The resort is a top-class tourist complex, complete with a marina, golf courses, a casino, hotels and luxury apartments. It is surrounded by broad, sandy beaches, well-tended gardens and examples of bold, innovative architecture.

As far back as the Romans, Vilamoura has been loved for its beauty: archaeological digs at **Cerro da Vila** have turned up the remains of a villa and public baths. Near the marina stands what is left of Loulé Velho, a tiny fishing village whose inhabitants were continually driven back by the ravages of the sea until in the end they gave up the struggle and settled inland. Until the 50s, when Armenian millionaire Calouste Gulbenkian bought the estate, Vilamoura was a mainly agricultural concern. There was a sizeable fish-farming operation, and clam beds were cultivated in the lagoons which form at the mouth of Ria Formosa.

Nowadays these installations have been replaced by the manicured lawns of golf courses, which stretch out to the neighbouring pine groves.

Ria Formosa, which takes in the coast of the Algarve from the beach at Falésia as far as Cacela, has been declared a nature reserve. It is home to a rich variety of ornithological life, and a major stopping-off point for migrant birds from the North. Efforts have been made to preserve the countryside hereabouts, with its particular mix of dunes, islets and creeks, by trying to maintain the ecological balance and take care that man-made features blend in with the landscape.

As well as being a meeting point for sailors from all around the world, Vilamoura's marina is also an international conference centre. Other attractions include the click of the roulette wheel and the glittering entertainment on offer at the casino, which is just one facet of Vilamoura's ever-lively nightlife.

With its enticing mix of glamour, sporting action, peaceful countryside and attractive beaches,

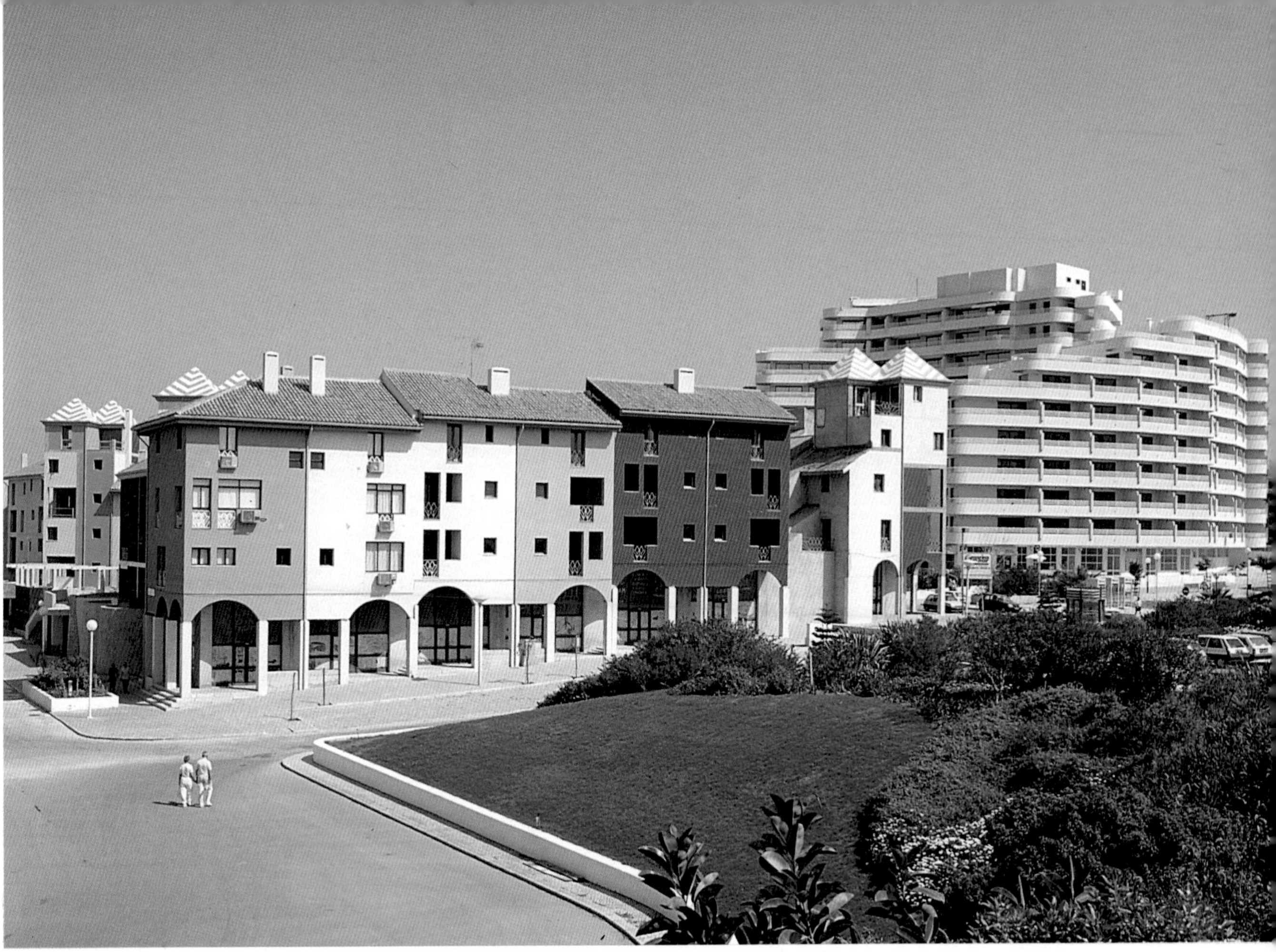

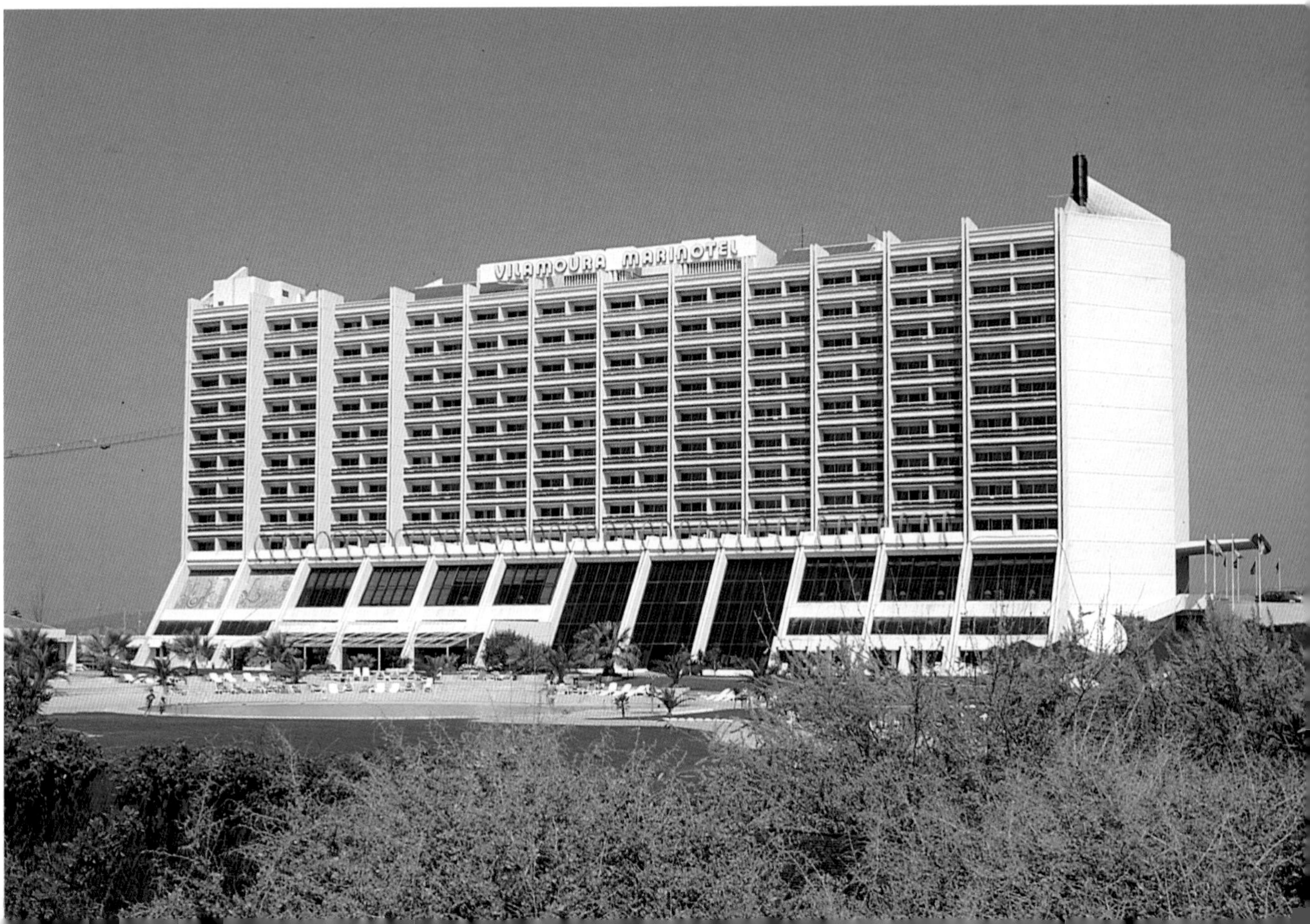
VILAMOURA MARINOTEL

Top class accomodation in one of Europe's largest holiday resorts

Golf and sporting facilities at Vilamoura

Vilamoura is an essential port of call for anyone visiting the Algarve. At the same time old habits die hard, and every night a row of lanterns can be seen bobbing all along the breakwaters which shelter the beach. They belong to the old-fashioned fishing boats which still haul in a nightly catch of fish and sea food to be enjoyed the following day in the resort's luxury hotels and beachfront cafés. Another surprise that Vilamoura holds in store for visitors is the variety of cooking on offer, ranging from Quarteira prawns and other traditional local dishes to the most exotic international cuisine.

Vilamoura's neighbour, **Quarteira**, is another former fishing village which has been transformed into a cosmopolitan tourist enclave, complete with wide, sunny avenues and pulsating nightlife. But walk just a little way out of town along the cliff tops to where the beach starts to unfold and you're back in the realm of limitless sand, emerald sea and gently breaking wavelets.

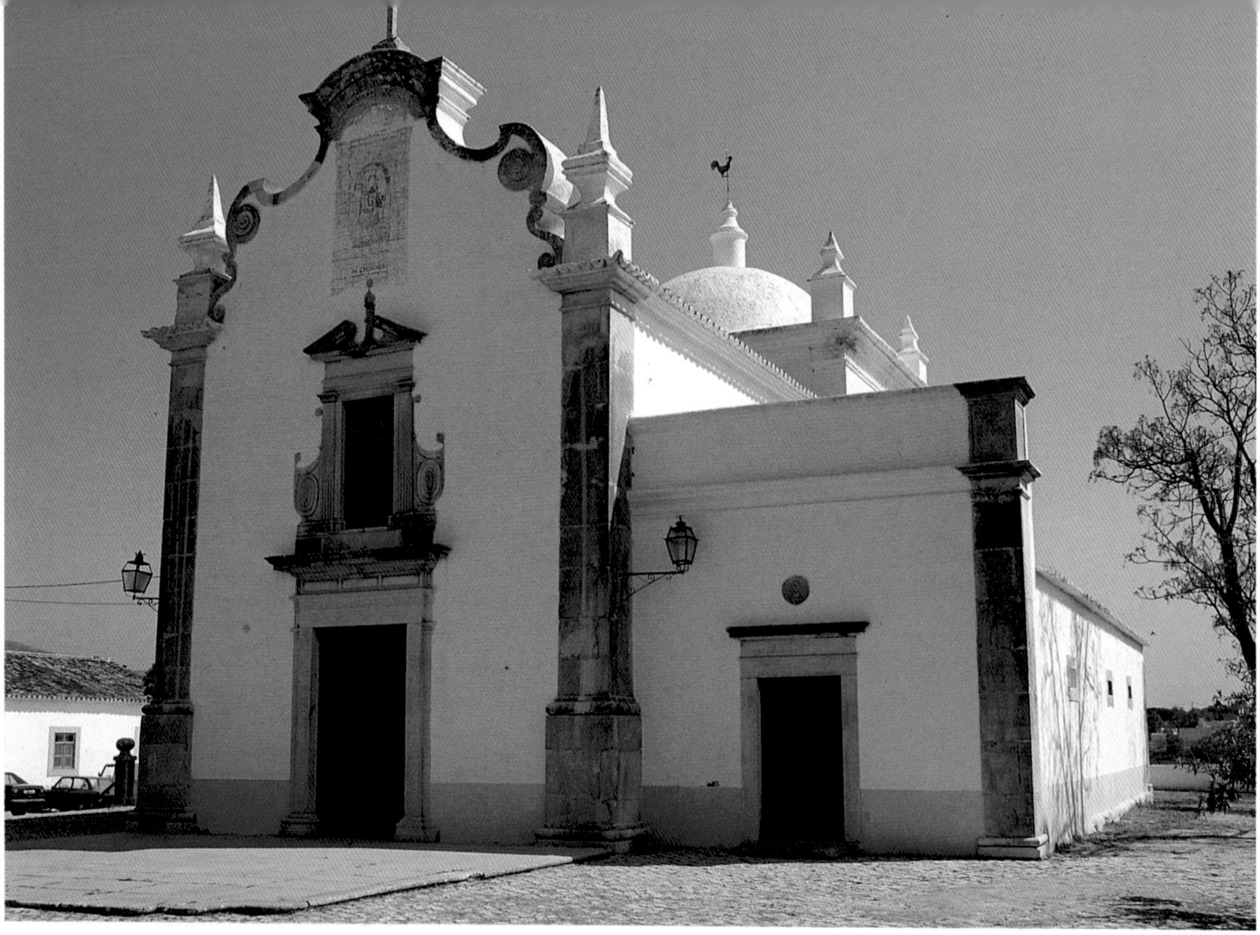

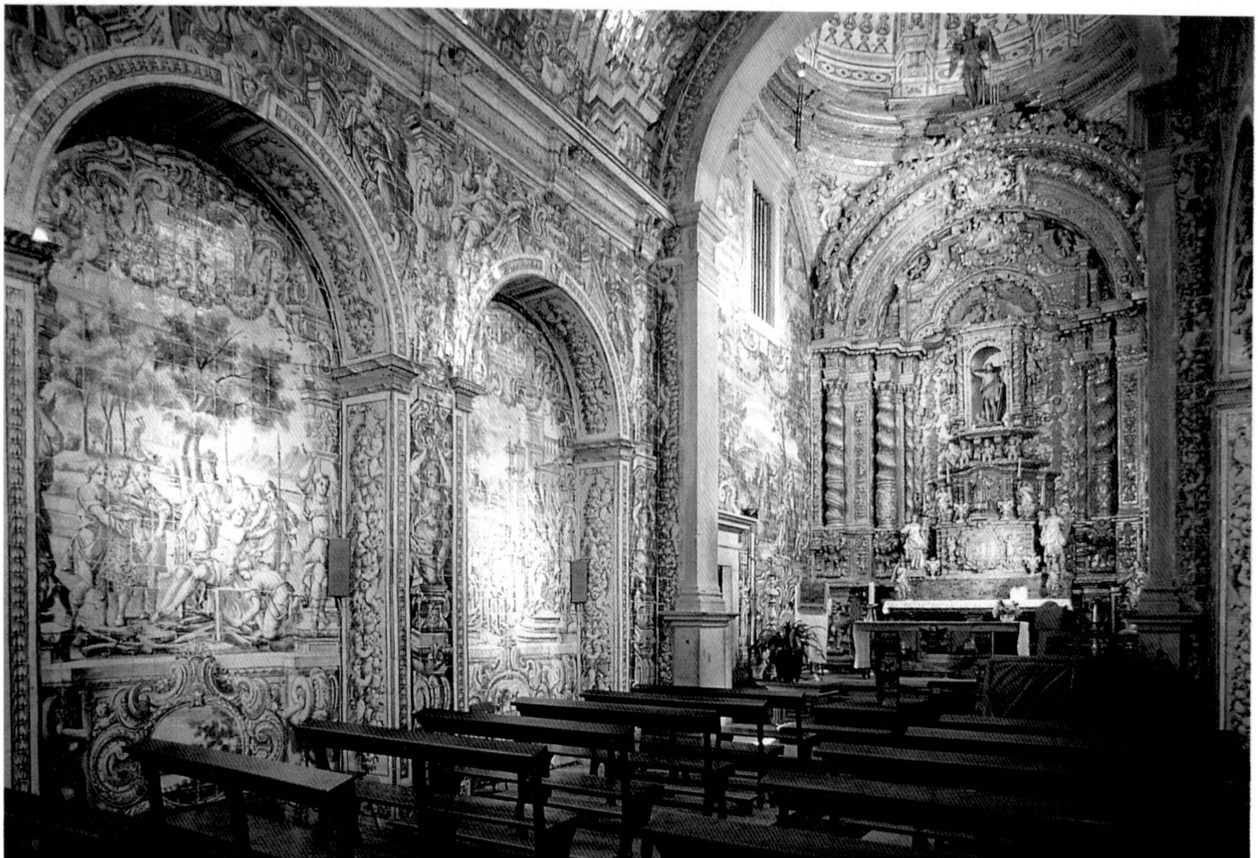

ALMANSIL

A small picturesque village, Almansil has maintained its tradition as a centre for crafts and handmade pottery and Algarve whitewash is still produced with traditional techniques. The **Centro Cultural** deserves a special visit; a country house restored and adapted to its new role, it includes an art gallery with a permanent exhibition of the sculptures of João Cutileiro, beautifully displayed in the garden.

SÃO LOURENÇO

São Lourenço, a small village a few miles from Almansil, boasts one of the prettiest churches in Portugal. It is completely covered with azulejos which date from 1730. The work of Policarpo de Oliveira Fernandes, the tiling which adorns walls, ceiling and cupola alike is a masterpiece of its kind. The tiles go well with the church's baroque architecture, and make a nice contrast with the gilded carving of the altar. Outside, there is a splendid view from the churchyard.

The Church of São Lourenço near Almansil

Remarkable azulejos panels line the interior of São Lourenço's

FARO

Faro lies at the heart of the Formosa estuary. The best way to arrive is by sea or air, to enjoy the full view of the sand and water, the labyrinth of marshland, islands and ocean inlets.

How this estuary was formed is a long story. Movements of the earth's crust, winds, tides, sediments washed from cliffs eroding to the west, and sands carried down from the mountains by the streams which here flow into the sea. Man has also had a hand, adapting as ever the natural lie of the land to his own needs. The estuary is constantly changing, as some channels are blocked and others opened, salt flats tended, nurseries built for shell fish and waters closed for feeding grounds for molluscs and a variety of different fish. The **Ria Formosa** is refashioned everyday. Faro, or *Óssonoba* for the Romans, was probably first founded for fishing and defence. Its present name comes from *Ben Said Ben Harun*, the Arab prince who es-

tablished the city state in 1031, under his short-lived principality.

The old town, is all that remains of distant times. A fishing village in pre-historic times, Faro became a trading post for the Phoenicians and Greeks, witnessed the splendour of the Roman empire and then saw Arab occupation and the founding of a principality. Faro survived historical and natural calamities, until in 1294 it was conquered by King Afonso III, who then proclaimed himself king of Portugal and the Algarves.

Through its association with members of the royal house Faro grew in importance and definitively supplanted Silves when the bishopric was moved there in 1540.

In 1596, the Count of Essex, favourite of Queen Elizabeth I of England, attacked and sacked the city at the front of 3000 men, leaving it in flames. Reborn from the ashes, Faro was rebuilt, only to be

The Paço Episcopal on Cathedral Square

52

The Cathedral (XIII century)

Statue of Dom Fancisco Gomes (1739-1816), Faro's most eminent citizen

razed to the ground in the earthquake of 1755. In 1808, under occupation from Junot's troops during the Napoleonic wars, the townspeople followed the example of other towns in the Algarve, and rebelled and turned out the invaders.

Faro was also the scene of disputes between liberals and Miguelists in the monarchical struggles of the early nineteenth century. Capital of the Algarve since 1756, the city has emerged from the vicissitudes of its history with the prosperity which befits its strategic and political importance.

Entering the town through the **Arco da Vila**, or city gate, which adjoins the Governor's Palace, a short walk uphill leads to the **Largo da Sé**, fronted by the cathedral. Only a tower, a door and two chapels remain of the old church built in 1251 on the site of the mosque. This in turn was built on the site of the primitive Gothic church and a Roman temple. The

53

present building shows no sign of the religious turn-arounds of the past.

What catches the eye are the subsequent alterations to the structure, with Gothic, renaissance and baroque elements all mixed together. Inside the cathedral is decorated with eighteenth century tiles, wood carvings inlaid with marble, some striking reliquaries, the organ and a precious incense-boat of silver and mother of pearl from the XVIII century.

The facade of the **Bishop's Palace**, which faces the cathedral, is covered with colourful azulejo panels produced at the Fábrica do Rato.

The old castle walls of Faro have been reduced with time to a few stretches which culminate in the **Arco do Repouso** which shelters a tiny votive chapel, traditionally associated with the conquest of the city from the Moors by King Afonso III.

Capela N.S. da Graça inside the Cathedral

Capela N.S. de Lurdes

Capela N.S. da Conceição

Capela Sagrado Coração de Jesus

"Flight into Egypt" in an outstanding azulejos panel

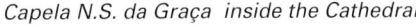

In front of the **Municipal Museum**, the statue of Afonso III dominates the perimeter of the ancient city. The museum is housed in the old **Convento de Nossa Senhora da Assunção** with its double cloister dating from 1543 around a quiet garden. The museum displays the Roman and Visigothic remains found in the city, Romanesque mosaics and tiles from down the ages.

The **Porta Nova** built on the site of the old Porta das Festas leads directly to the modern city. Here, on the way to the **Manuel Bivar Garden**, stands the Manueline **Igreja da Misericórdia**, adjoining the Hospital founded in 1795 by the Bishop D. Francisco Gomes Avelar. The colonnades and arches may be modest, but they offer a striking contrast with the modern design of the surrounding houses. In the Baroque **Igreja do Carmo** gilt wood carvings brighten the otherwise sombre nave, dating from 1719. The church possess works by Cristobal Gomez (1595) and the statue of the patron saint is attributed to the master sculptor Machado de Castro.

Clock tower and walls at Arco da Vila (XVIII century)

City Hall

Castle walls near Rua do Castelo

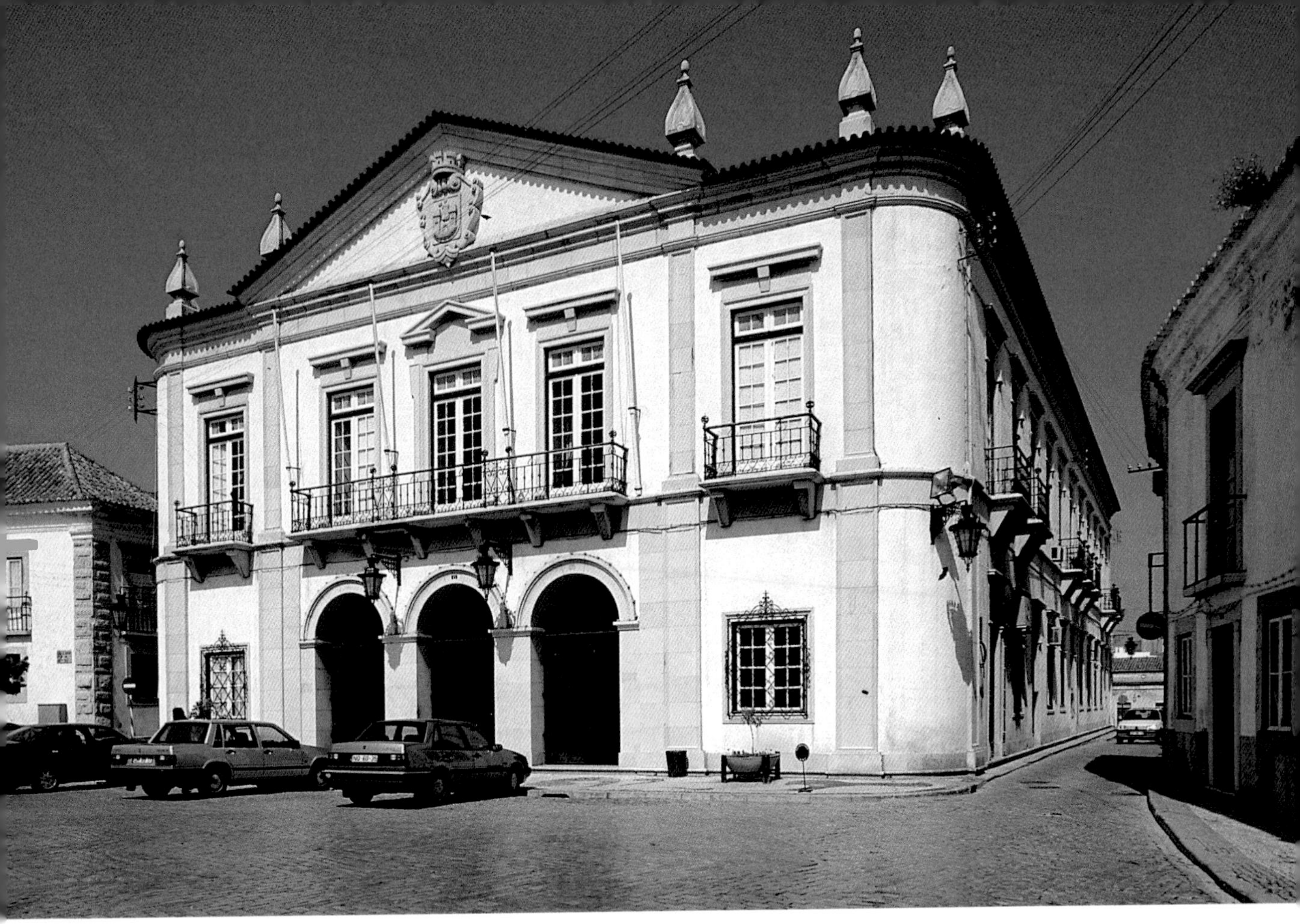

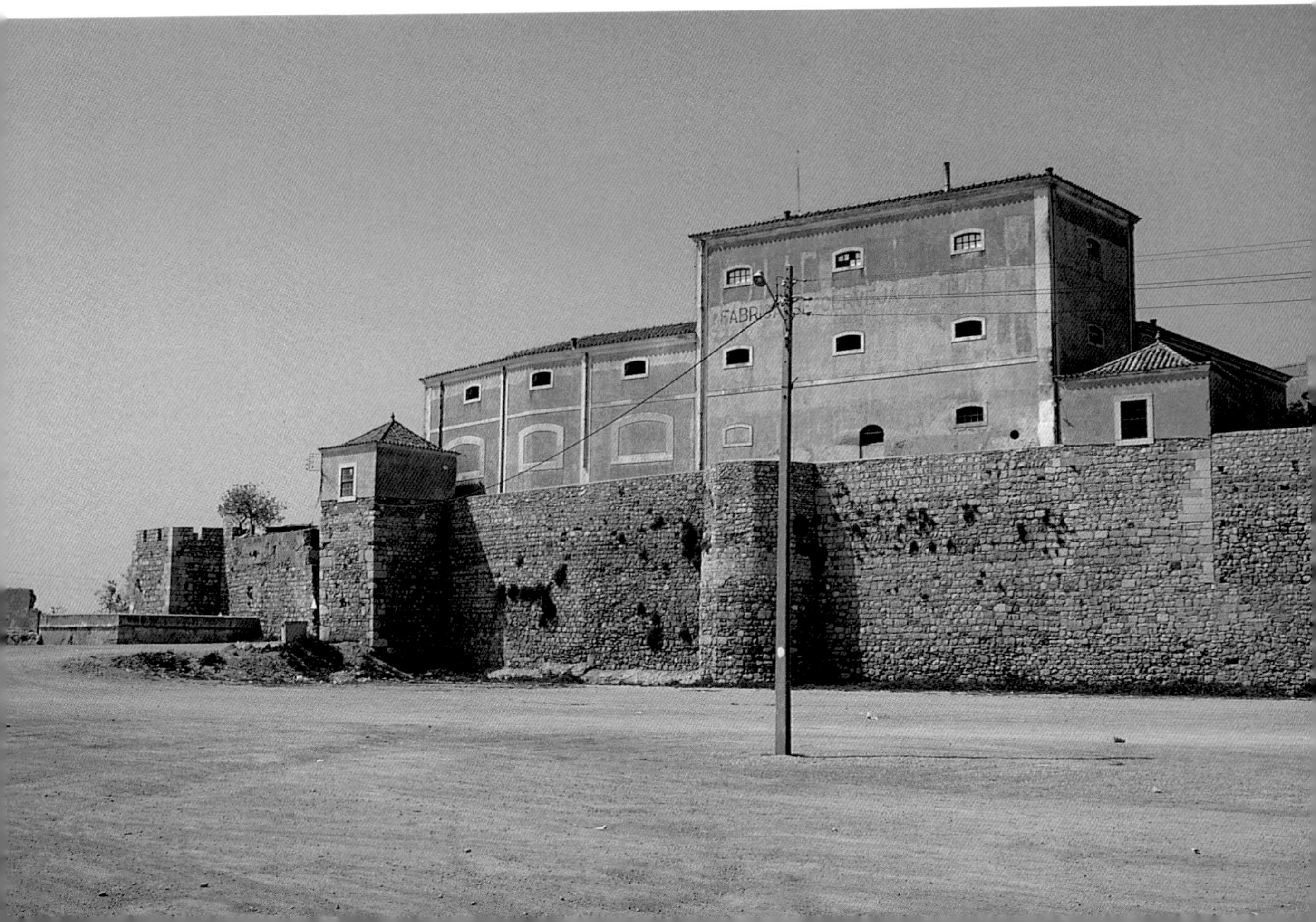

The nearby **Folk and Regional Museum** is wholly given over to the secular arts and crafts of the Algarve people, with a comprehensive display of full-size and miniature reproductions of traditional tools, traditional houses and regional dress. The sea runs in the blood of this people, and has brought them glory and disaster. The **Ramalho Ortigão Maritime Museum** houses reproductions of boats used down the centuries, as well as fishing tackle, maps and sea charts. The collection is complemented by a display of the most common marine species in the region.

In the **Largo de S.Francisco** the breeze rises from the estuary which, though unseen, pervades the city atmosphere. At the end of the promenade stands the XVI century **Igreja de S.Francisco**, with a simple nave and chancel. Nearby in the **Monastery of S.Francisco** there is a curious hexagonal granary with mythological figures depicted in bas relief.

Facade and interior of the XVIII century Igreja do Carmo

Igreja de São Francisco (XVI century)

Igreja de Sto. António do Alto (XVII century)

Visitors who walk out of the town along the Olhão road are rewarded with the view of the channels and lagoons of the Formosa from the **Miradouro de Santo António**. Here too is the **Antonine Museum**, adjoining the Hermitage of Santo António do Alto, containing a worthy collection of images, books and engravings of the life of Saint Anthony. Interestingly, printing in Portugal was pioneered in Faro. In 1487, the Jew Samuel Gacon printed the Pentateuch in his workshop, the oldest Portuguese incunabula.

Rapid urban development looks set to swallow up what remains of traditional architecture, but in some corners of the city there are still narrow picturesque streets with sash windows and wrought iron balconies. The S.Pedro quarter, built in the XVII century around the church of the same name, remains true to the style of the time. And the facades of the Belmarço and Bivar palaces speak of the secrets of the ancient city.

VALE DO LOBO

Vale do Lobo's recent expansion is closely tied up with the game of golf and the habits of the international jet set, who regularly flee the rigours of winter in northern Europe to take advantage of the Algarve's mild climate. Another attraction is the possibility of swapping the bustle of Europe's capitals for the calm of green lawns and pretty seaside scenery. Looking out over the cliffs, the houses resemble steamships at anchor, ready to set sail at any moment.

The growing popularity of watersports has added to Vale do Lobo's appeal, and yachts can be seen tacking alongside windsurfers, while young enthusiasts ride up and down on jetskis.

View of the beach at Vale do Lobo

One of the Henry Cotton designed golf courses at Vale do Lobo

Moorish style villas set amongst pinewoods

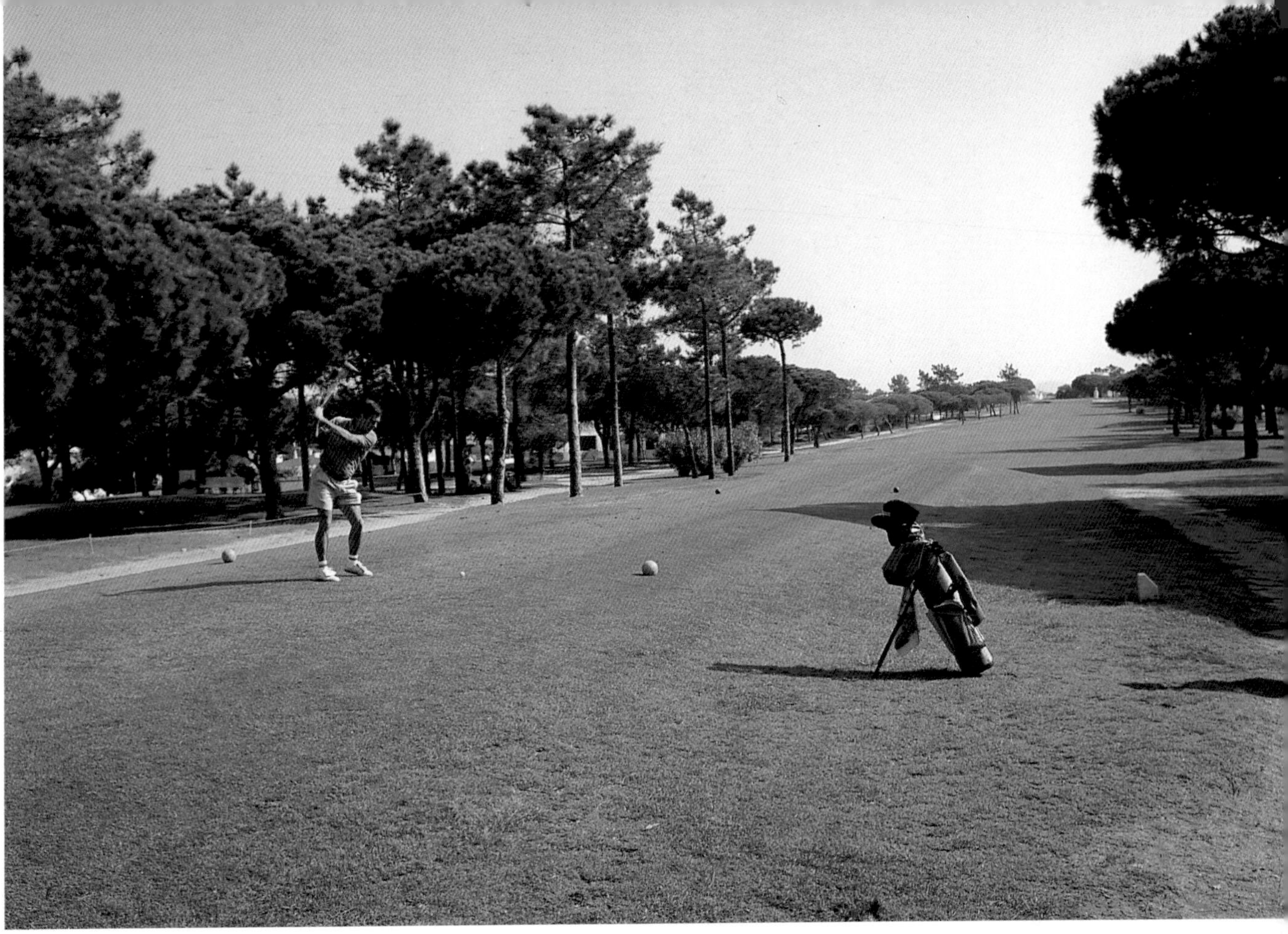

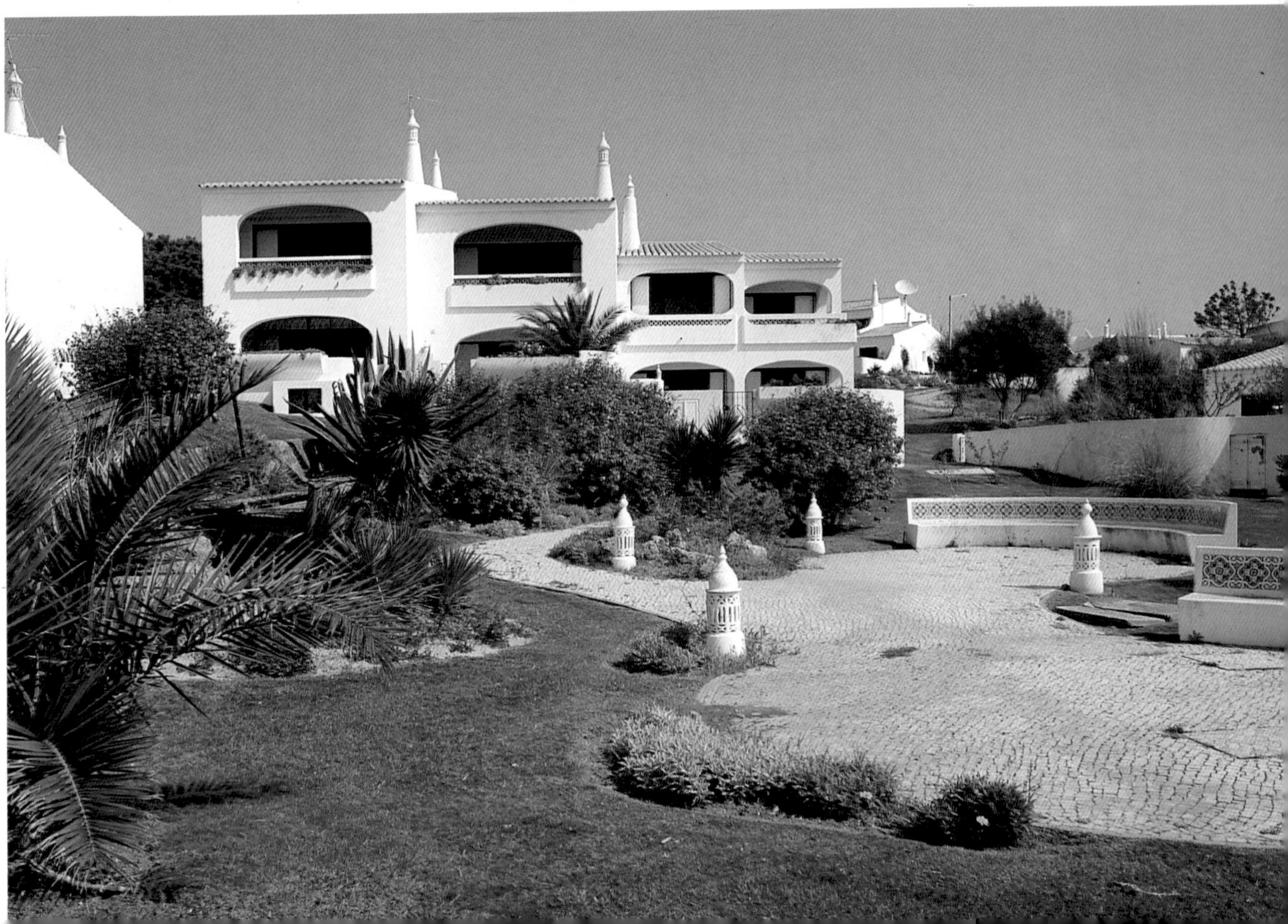

The development has its own shopping centre and there is a lively night life based around the discotheques and nightclubs, all of which have been designed so as not to disturb the tranquillity of those who come to play sport during the day and take it easy in the evening.

The huge pine wood which surrounds Vale do Lobo gives the whole area a feeling of peace and closeness to nature, an impression heightened by the reed beds of **Ribeira de Almargem**, which are a nesting ground for many rare species of bird. As far as scenery goes, Vale do Lobo's appeal lies mainly in its beaches, which form a wide bay, from which the houses of Albufeira are visible as a white strip on one side and the town of Quarteira on the other.

Golf course

Kiosk and shopping facilities

Golf course overlooking the Atlantic

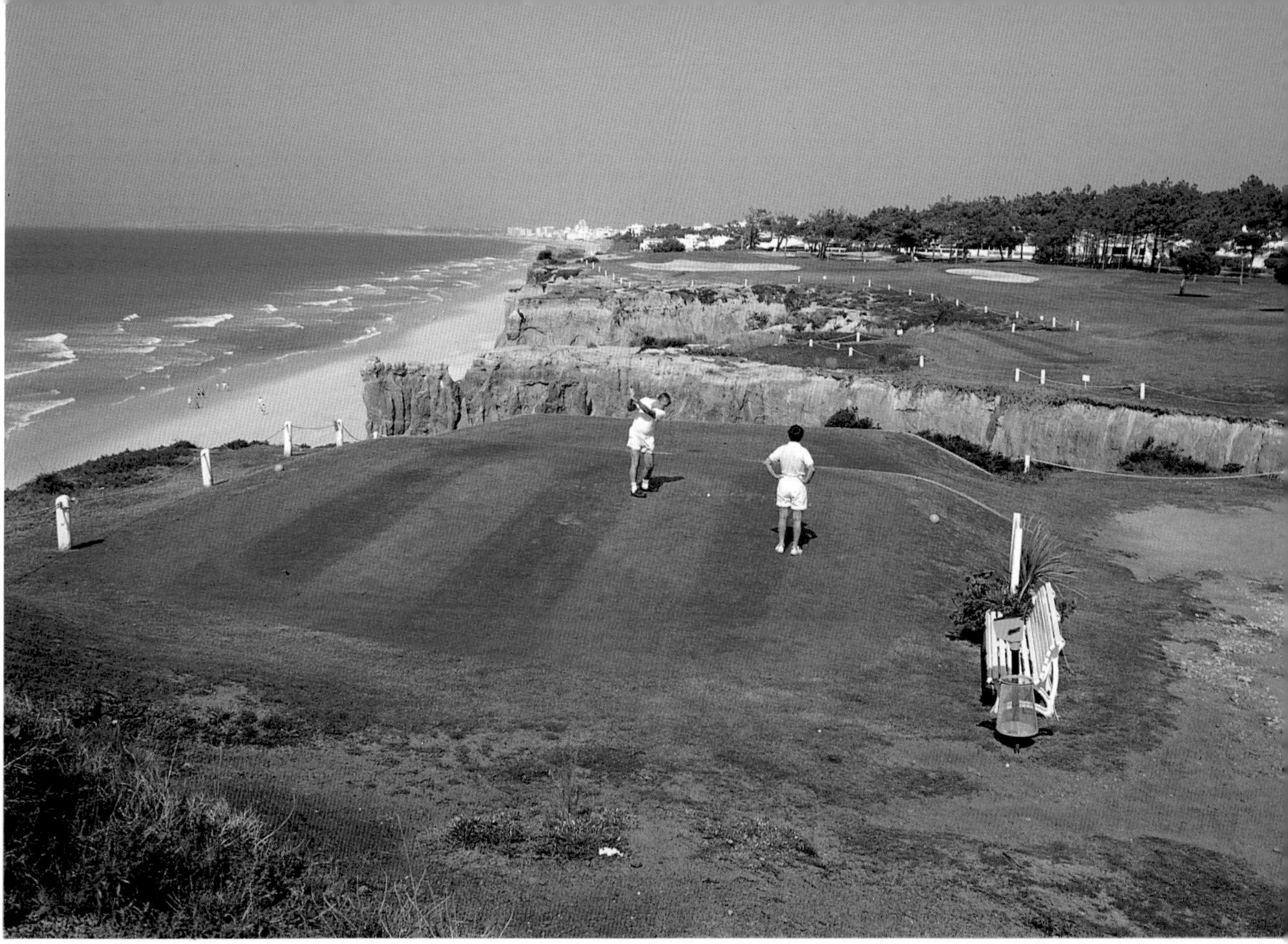

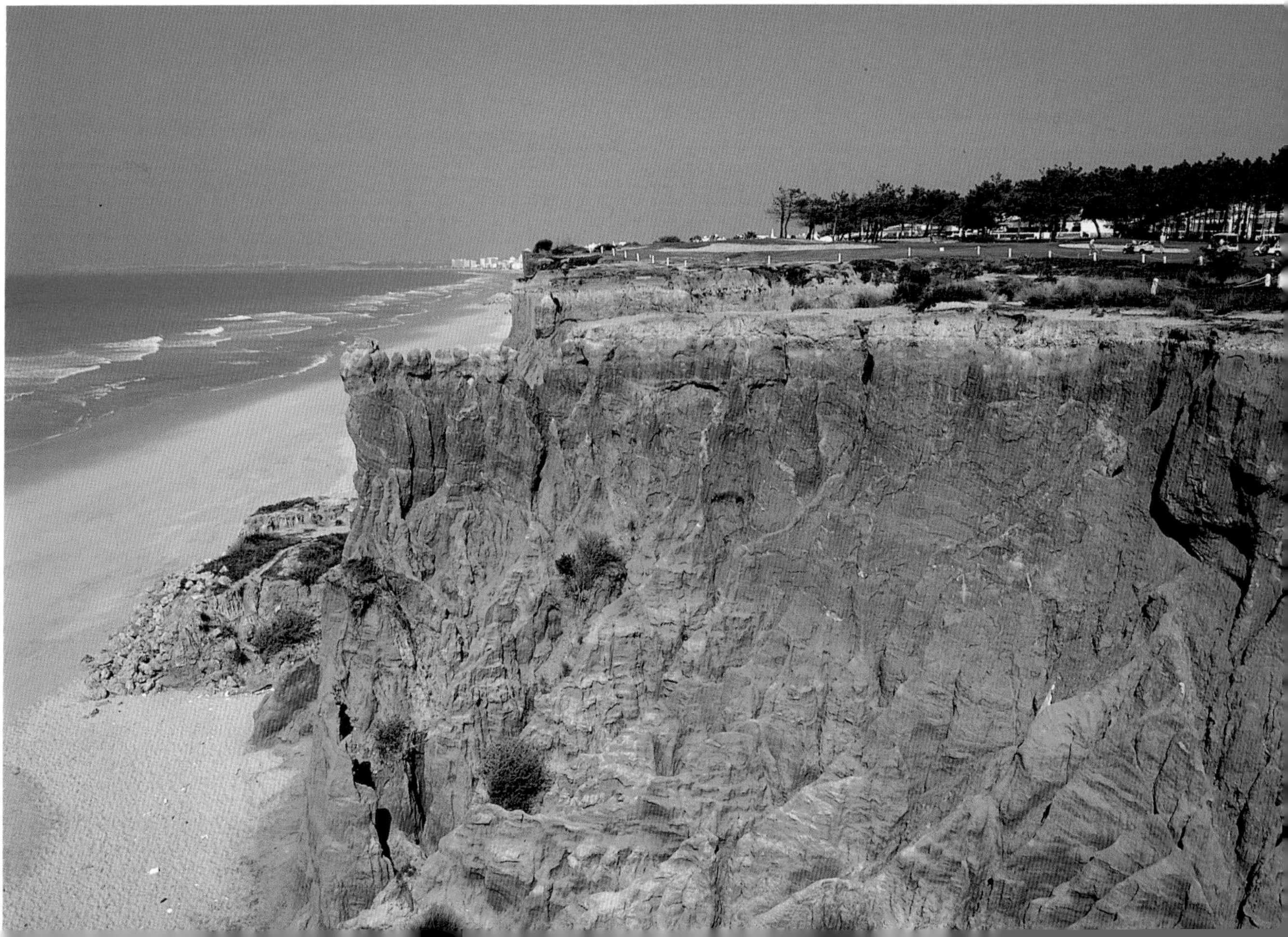

Inlet at Quinta do Lago

Club house and golfing facilities at Quinta do Lago

QUINTA DO LAGO

At the mouth of the **Ria Formosa**, **Quinta do Lago** is a paradise of contrasts, with wide strands and rolling dunes, the streams and lagoons of the Nature Reserve. Designed for a highly select clientele, almost nowhere else in the Algarve has greater care been taken in preserving the beauty of the landscape or in adding to the contrasting charms of nature. The remains of Arabic buildings show that this landscape has been loved for centuries. The Romans also left behind signs of their presence, and the remains of a farm house and adjoining baths can be seen, and an archeological rarity - tanks for salting fish, probably caught in the channels of the Ria Formosa which still today abound in fish and seafood.The spreading green branches of umbrella pines offer shade from the burning sun on the golf course which winds between the pine woods, lagoons and grassy fields. Riding and tennis are also popular at Quinta do Lago, together with water sports on the largest of the lagoons.

For those who prefer to come out at night, Quinta do Lago's recreational facilities include one of the largest discotheques in the country, with capacity for 4 thousand. Next door is the luxurious **T Club**, built in Arabian style with wide interior patios and spreading verandahs, frequented by Portuguese and

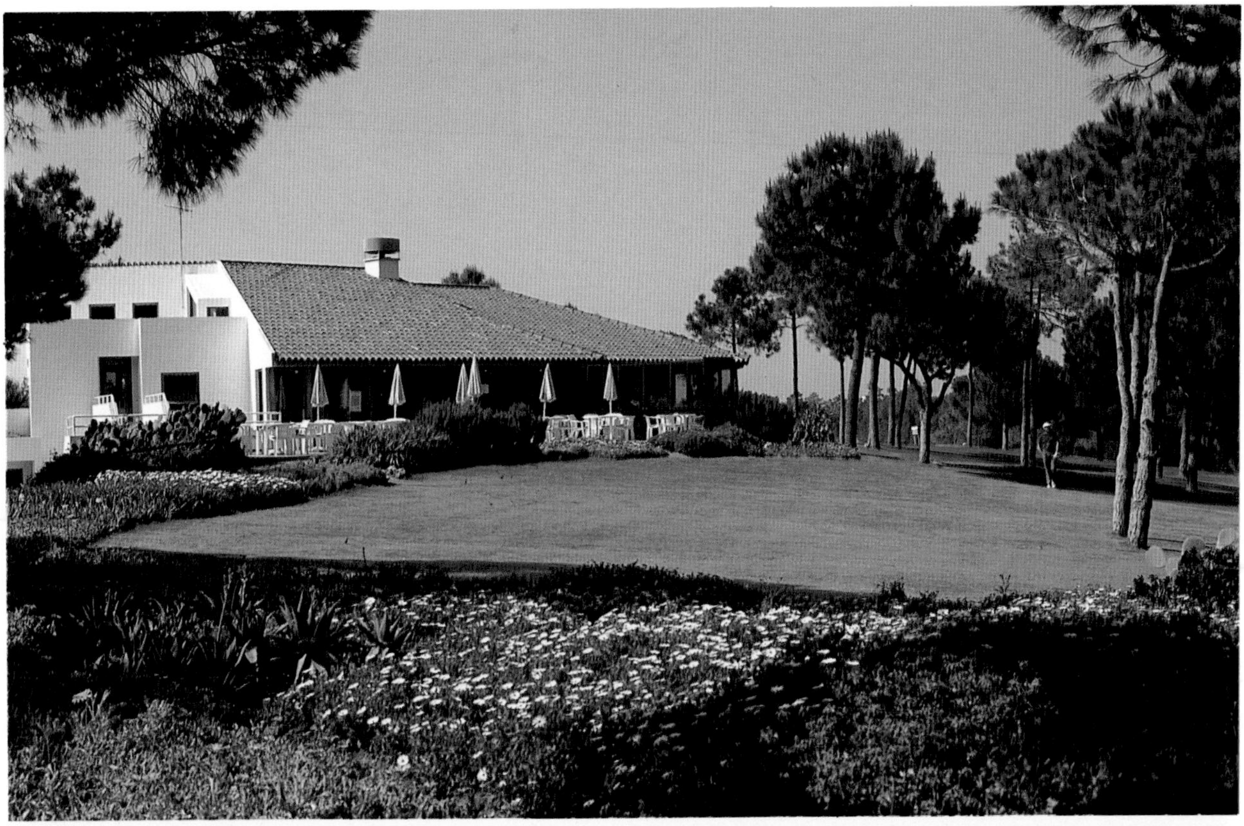

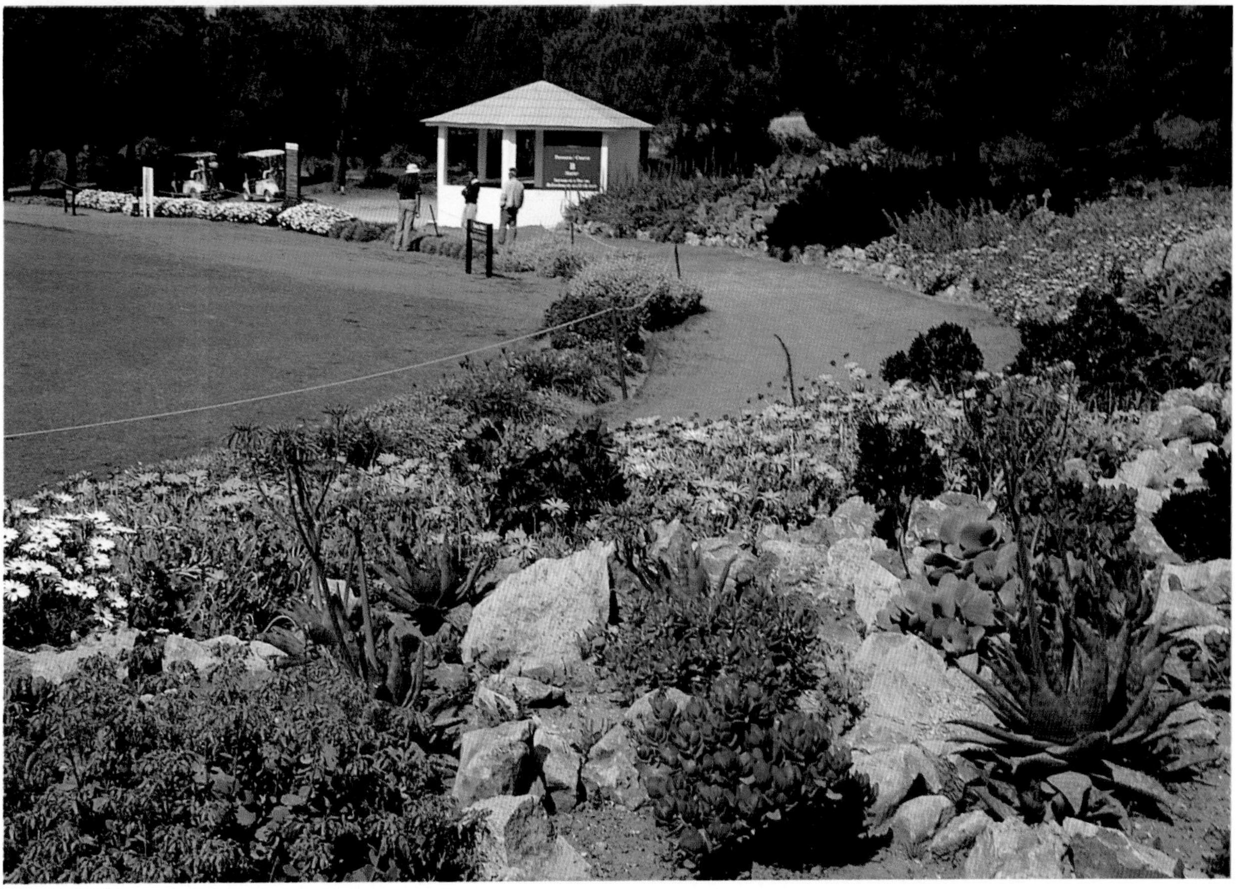

The 27 hole golf course is regularly used for the Portuguese Open Championships

Riding at Quinta do Lago

Wooden causeway

foreign politicians. In the pursuit of absolute privacy and discretion, the accommodation in Quinta do Lago is in houses hidden behind leafy gardens, complete with private swimming pools and tennis courts.

Blending perfectly into the varied landscape of this area, Quinta do Lago combines sophistication with the unique natural wonders of the Algarve.

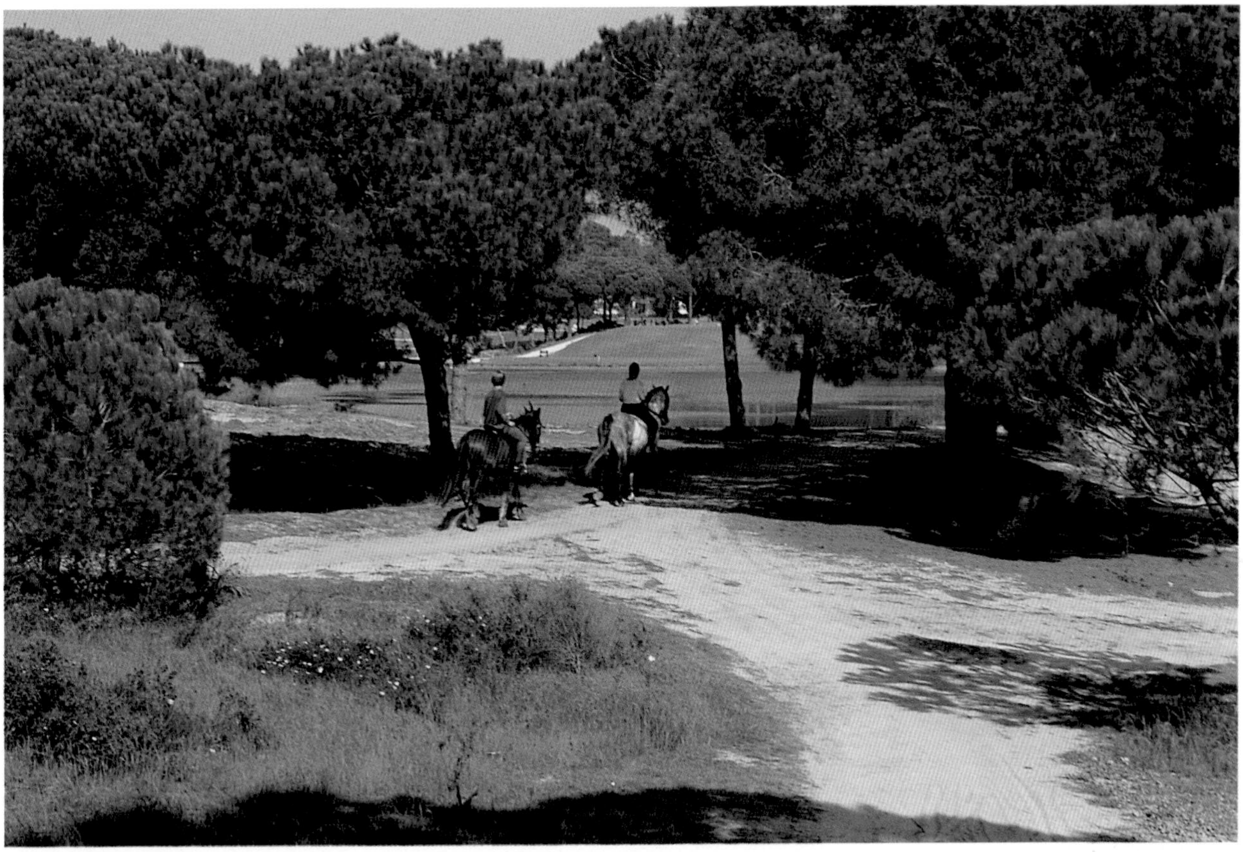

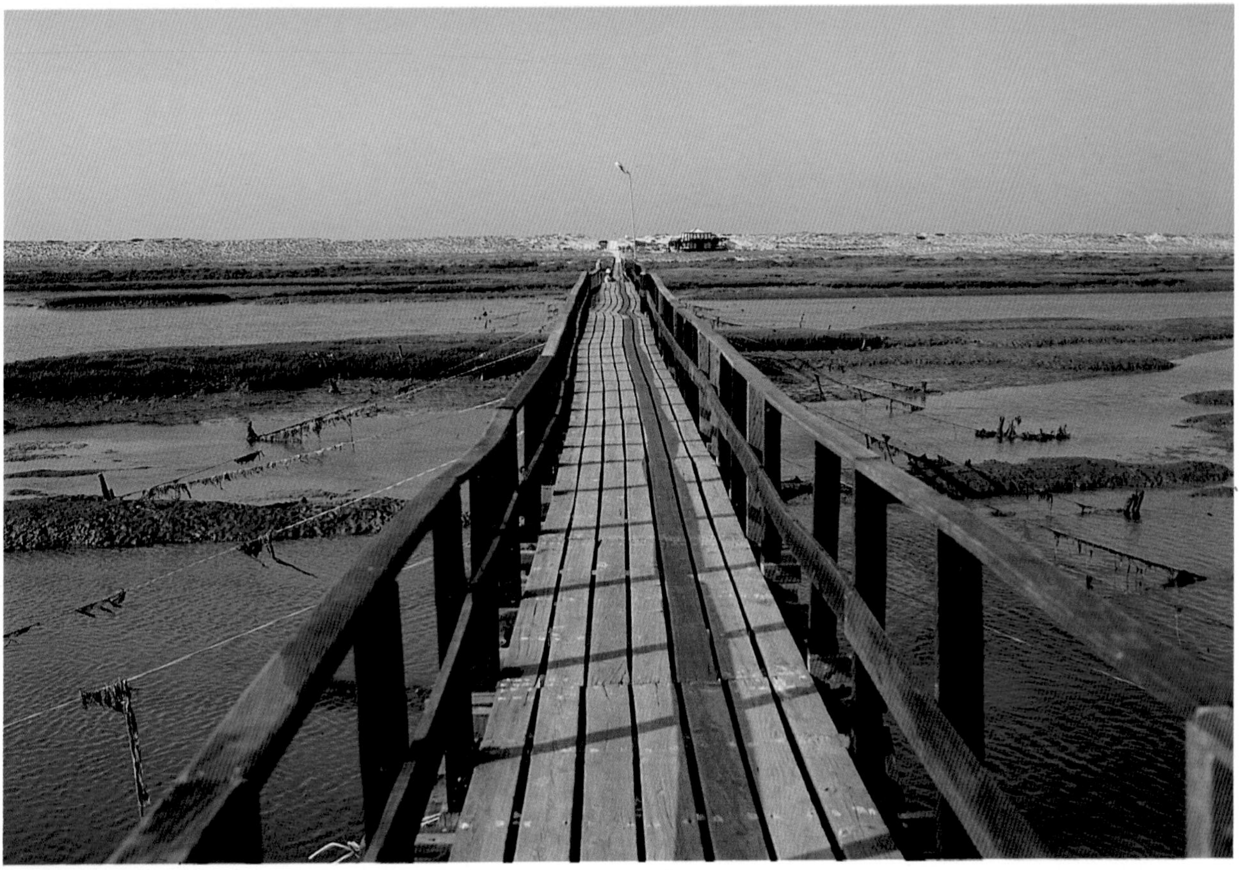

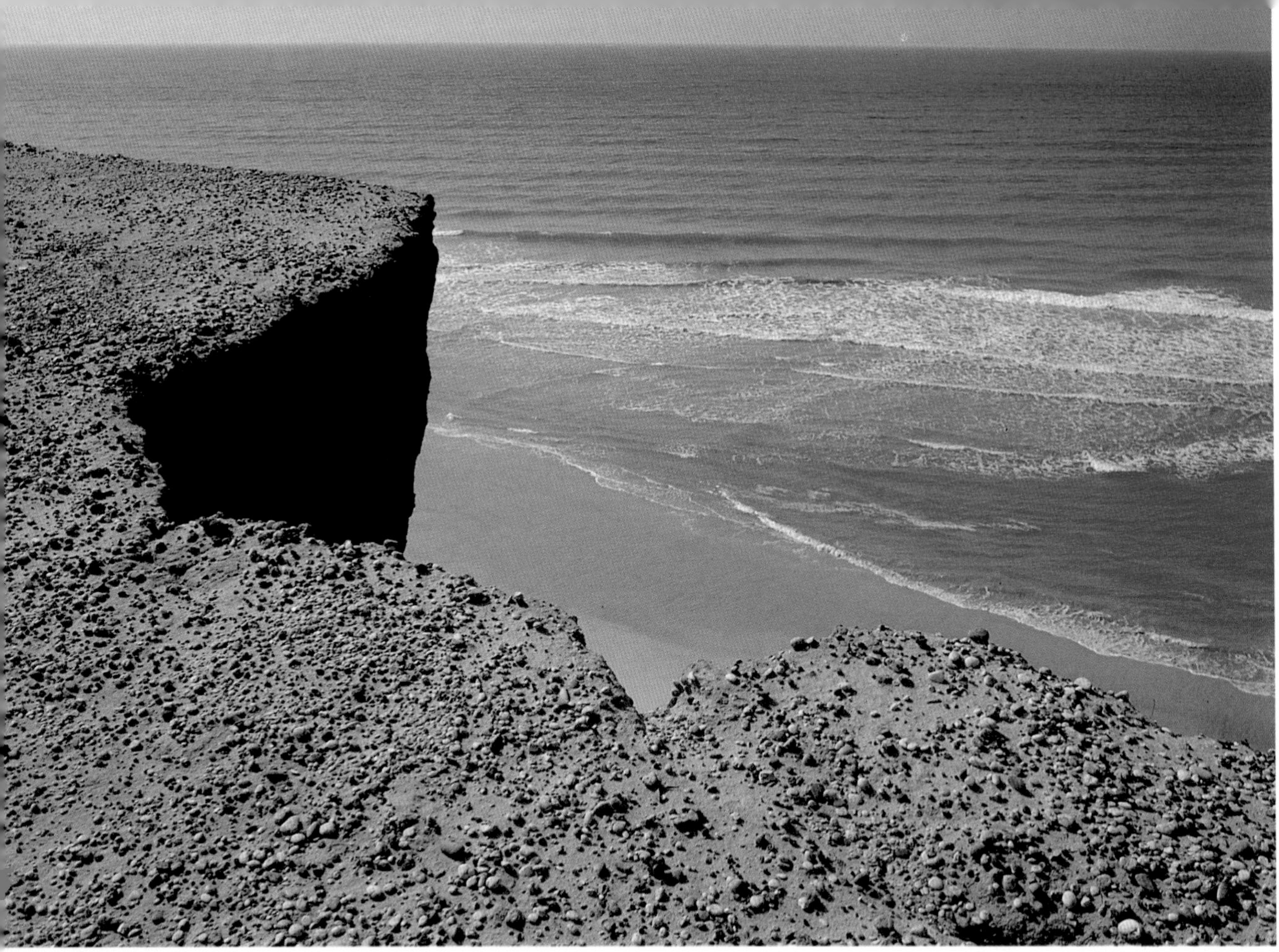

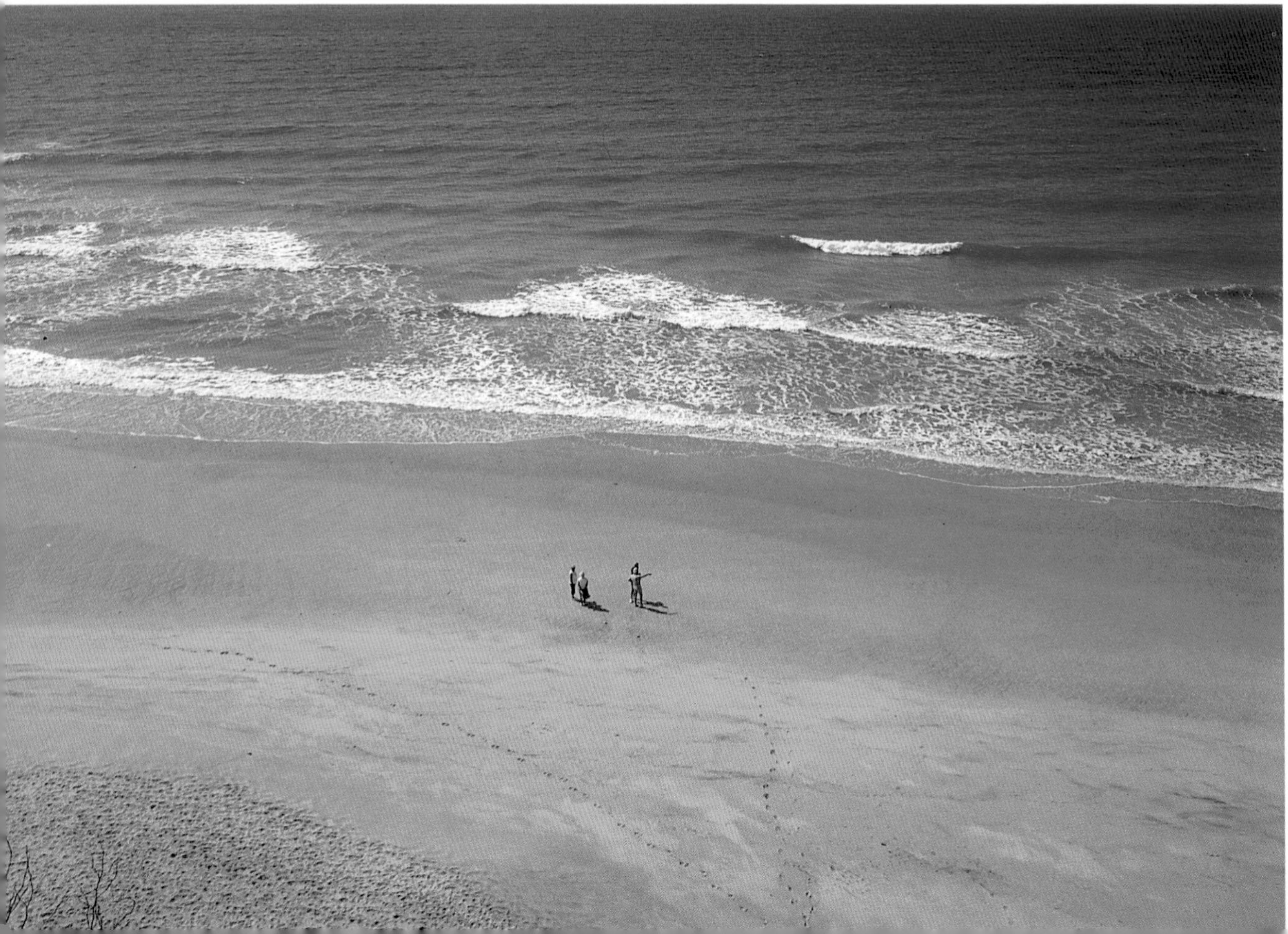

LOULÉ

The district of Loulé abounds in tiny villages like Querença, Salir, Barranco do Velho, Alte or Ameixal, each of which a perfect example of traditional Algarve building styles. In the uplands and hills the houses are built with rooftop terraces, patterned chimneys and *platibandas* - decorated stucco fascias. Almond trees standing in tiled patios, whitewashed walls in the sun.

Although we cannot be sure of who first settled in Loulé, Roman remains have been found and the town walls which weave in and out of the houses probably date back to the Arab occupation in the X century. The **Church of Saint Francis** contains a curious tabernacle in the form of a pelican and rich gilded wood carvings.

The traditional houses around the wall have been restored and now house the **Municipal Museum** and an arts centre. The XIII century **Parish Church** near to the historic heart of the town, with its curious columns and capitals, and the renaissance **Capela das Almas**.

On the roads leading to the town, mule drawn carts are a common sight, with wooden wheels painted yellow and the sides of the carts painted blue. In the centre of Loulé, near the market, tradition is retained and craftsmen work in their doorways, work-

Views of the long sandy beach at Quinta do Lago

The partially restored castle

ing on harnesses, beating copper and weaving baskets.

The Quinta dos Álamos and the Quinta do Rosil are fine examples of agricultural development in the nineteenth century. Terraces run down the upland slopes, retained by dry stone walls.

In the church of the outlying village of Salir the locals have preserved a precious and illuminated papal bull issued in 1550 by Pope Paul III. In **Barranco do Velho** stands an imposing olive tree which spreads more than 25 metres, measuring more than 15 metres high. The nearby rustic church looks all the more modest in comparison to the natural domes and arches of the ancient tree.

View of the town from the castle walls

A Moorish style structure houses the market at Loulé

A fountain and well in old Loulé

On the following pages:
The Capela das Almas in the XIII century Parish Church

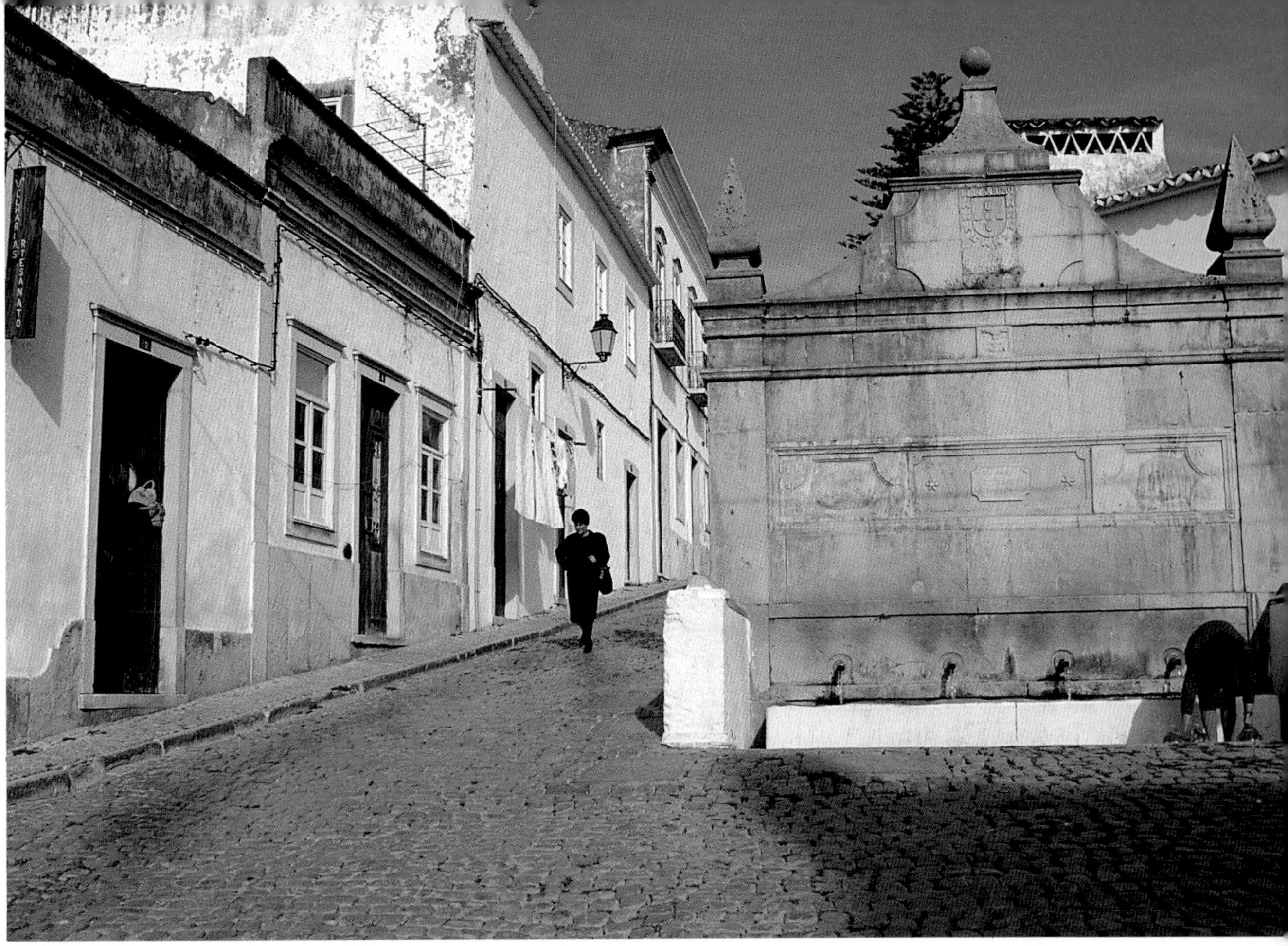
RTESANATO

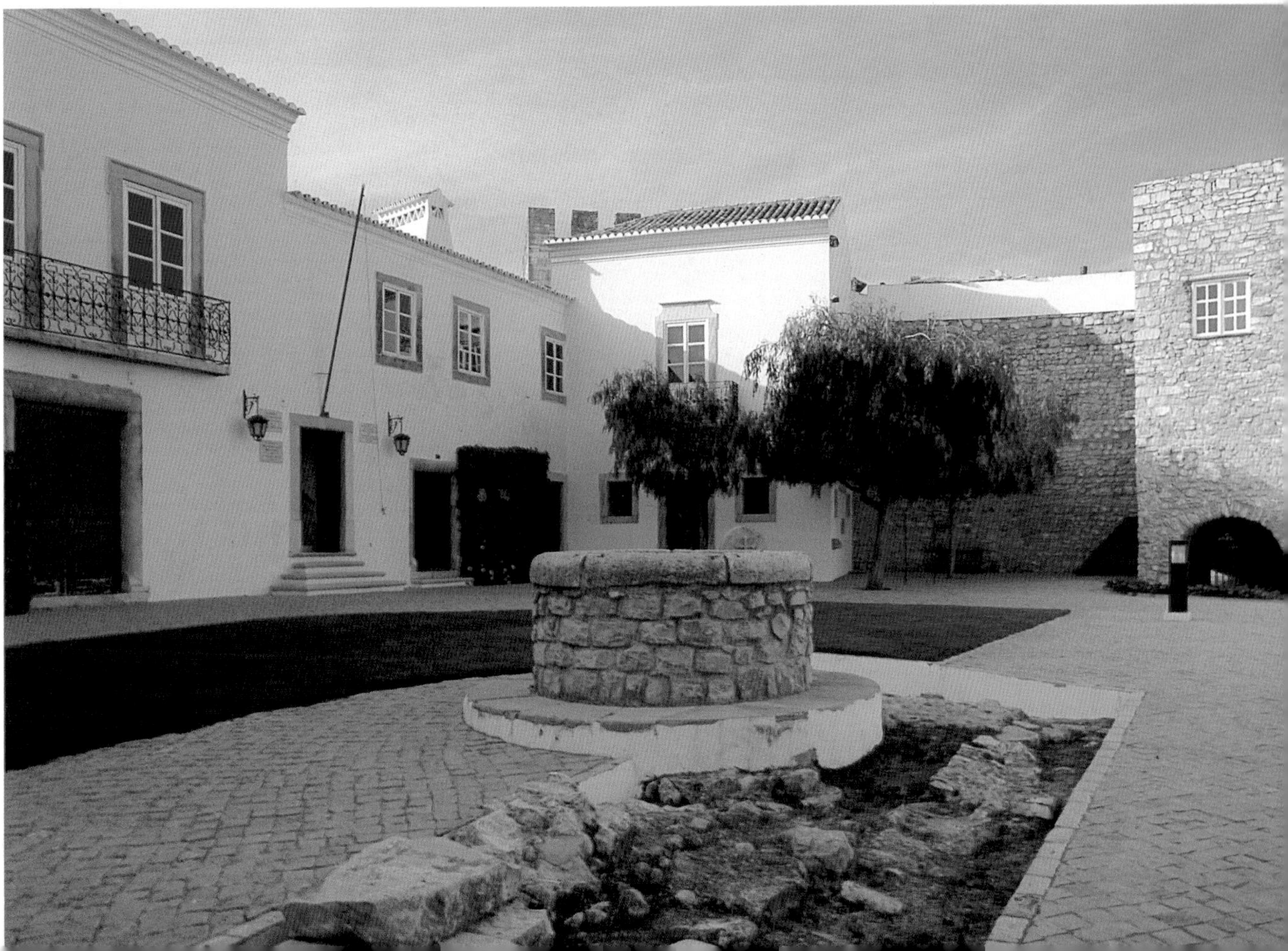

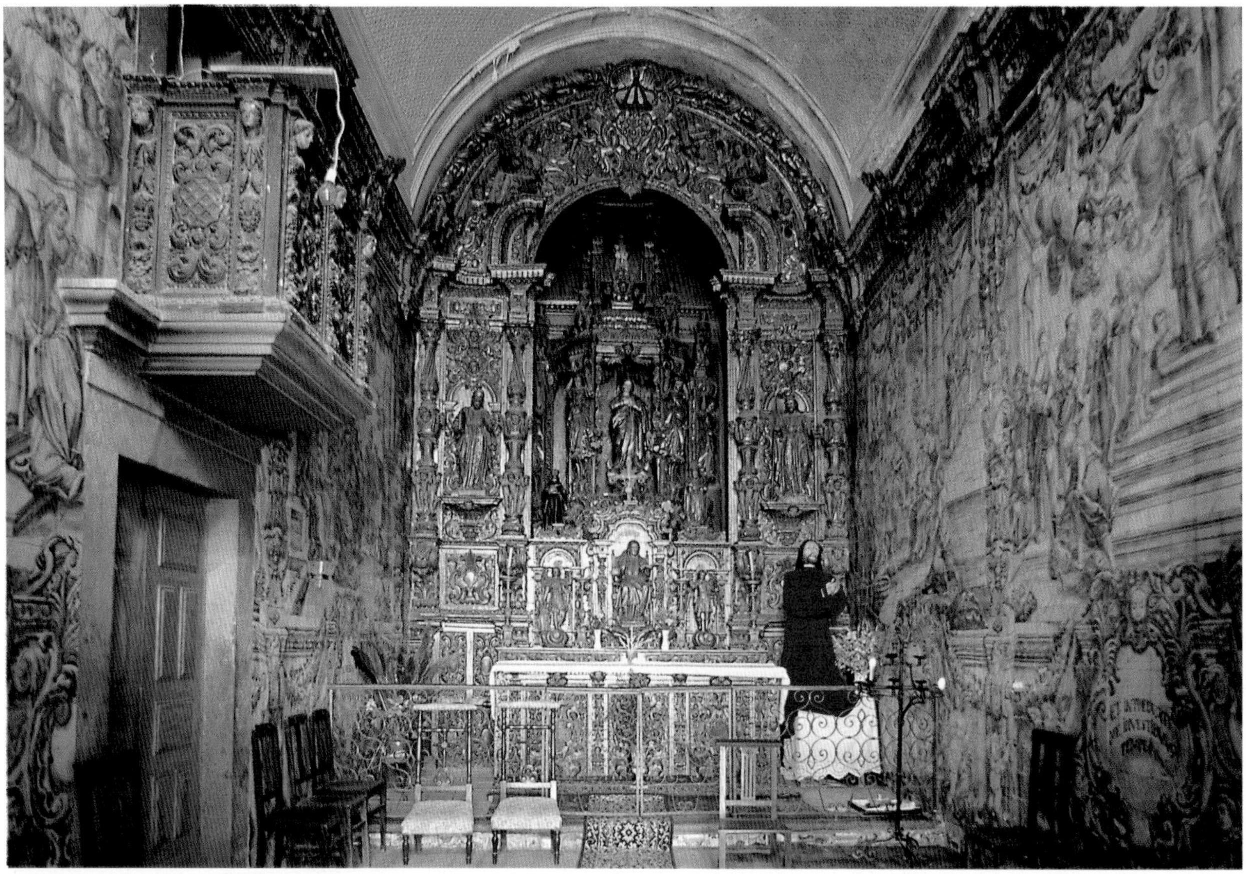

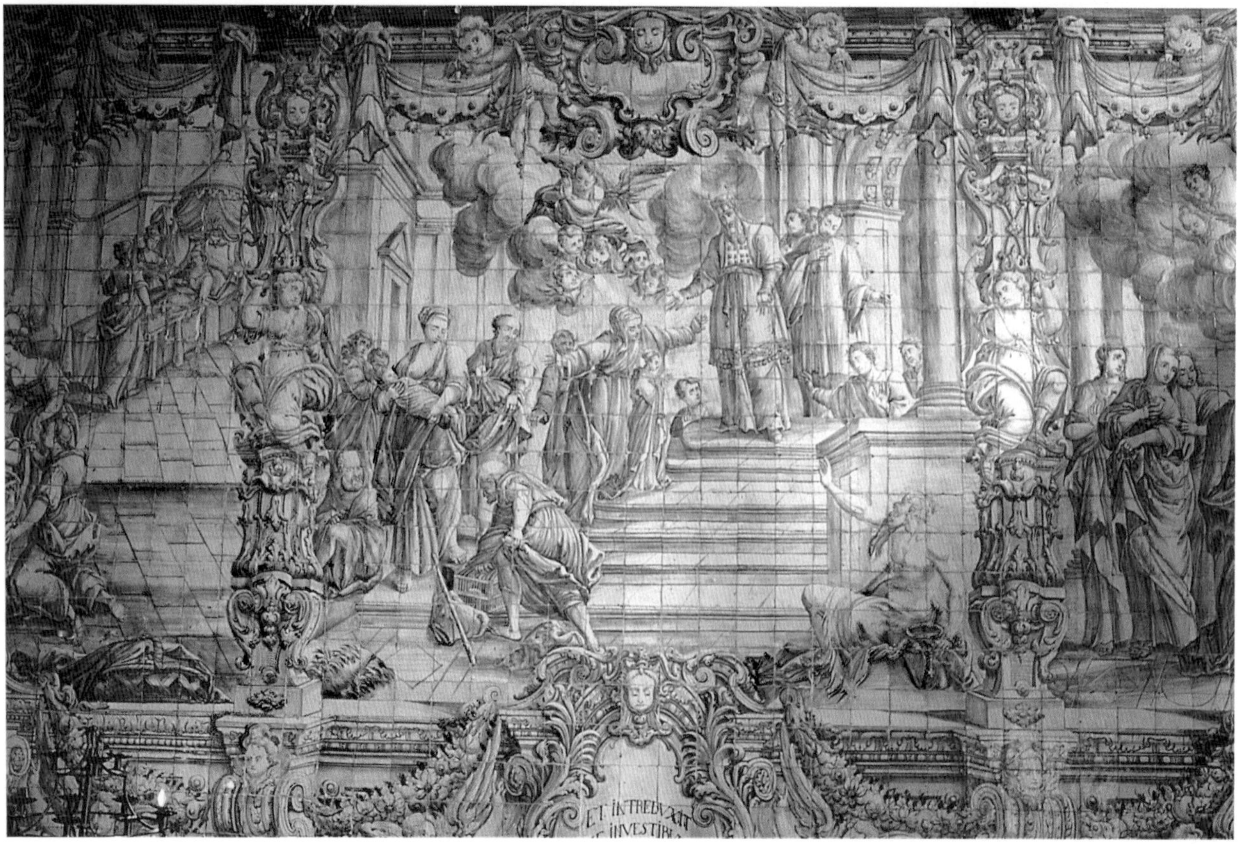

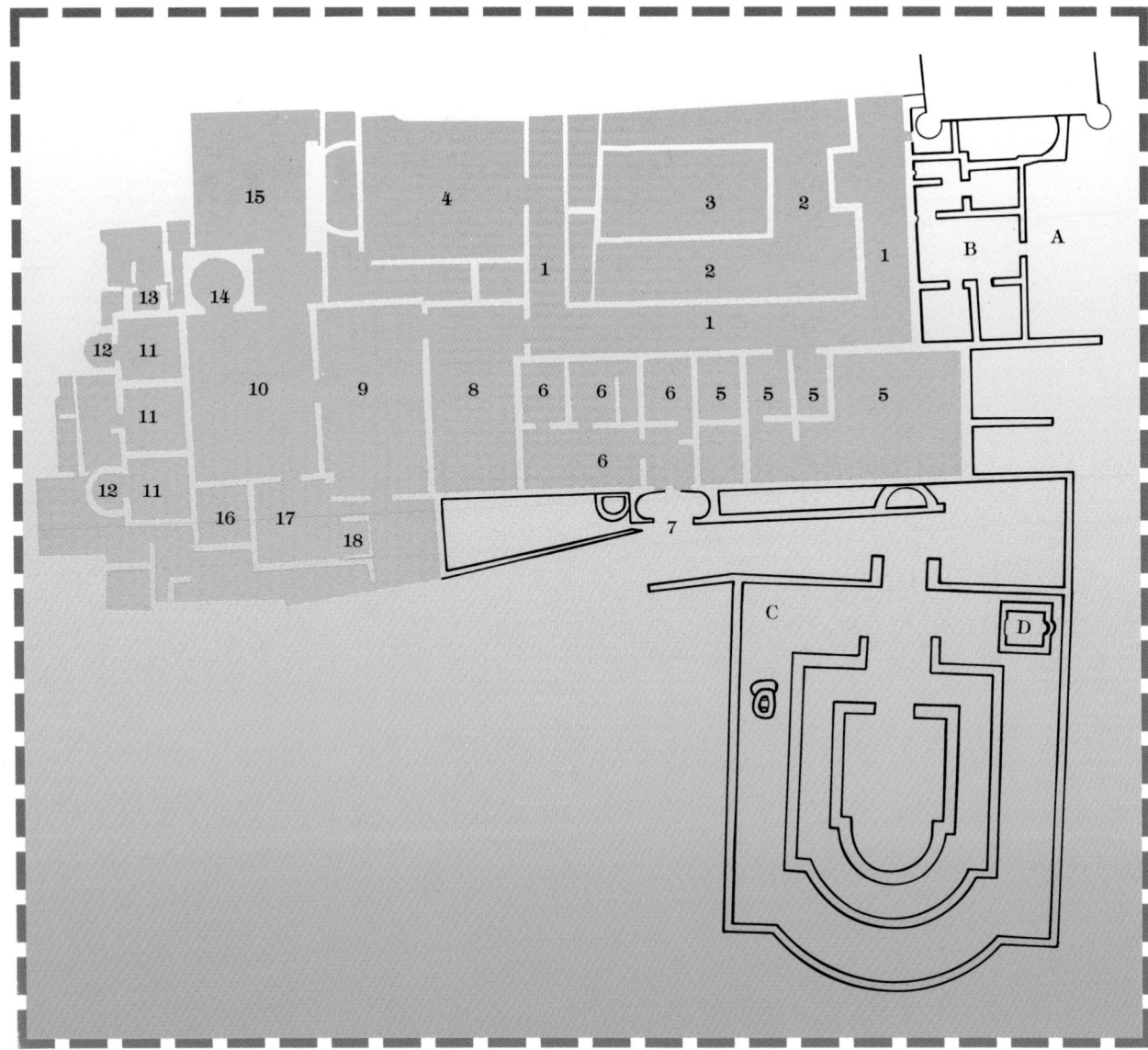

Plan of the Roman Villa

Legend

A — Water fountain
B — Chambers

1 — Peristyle
2 — Garden of the peristyle
3 — Pool of the peristyle
4 — Hall with an apse ("triclinium")
5 — Rooms accessible through the peristyle
6 — Rooms accessible through the main entrance
7 — Main entrance
8 — Baths' entrance hall
9 — "Apodyterium" (dressing room)

10 — "Frigidarium"
11 — "Calidarium" and "tepidarium"
12 — Pools of the "calidarium"
13 — "Praefurnium"
14 — Pool of the "frigidarium"
15 — Room (gymnasium?)
16 — "Tepidarium"
17 — "Frigidarium" (women?)
18 — Pool with mosaics representing fishes

C — Baptismal pool
D — Mausoleum

The Temple, baths and living areas

MILREU

When the Romans arrived in the Algarve, in the first century B.C., they set about reorganising the territory and its agriculture.

Farming was centred around *villae rusticae* which by the second century A.D. had grown to an impressive size compared to the small and functional houses first built. Milreu is an example of such a *villa rustica*, a large house decorated with considerable luxury, including marble, mosaics and an efficient water supply system.

The identity of the Roman patrician who built the house and farmed the land around remains a secret of the gods, but his family was undoubtedly wealthy. Some of the mosaics are in gold and two large mausoleums have been found, as well as busts of Agrippina, Hadrian and Gallienus, members of the imperial Roman household.

Milreu was discovered in 1877 by the Algarve archeologist, Estácio da Veiga. The residential quarters of the villa have been excavated although conservation works have yet to be completed. The baths, temple and living areas can be clearly seen. More recent excavations inside a farm building dating from the beginning of this century have revealed

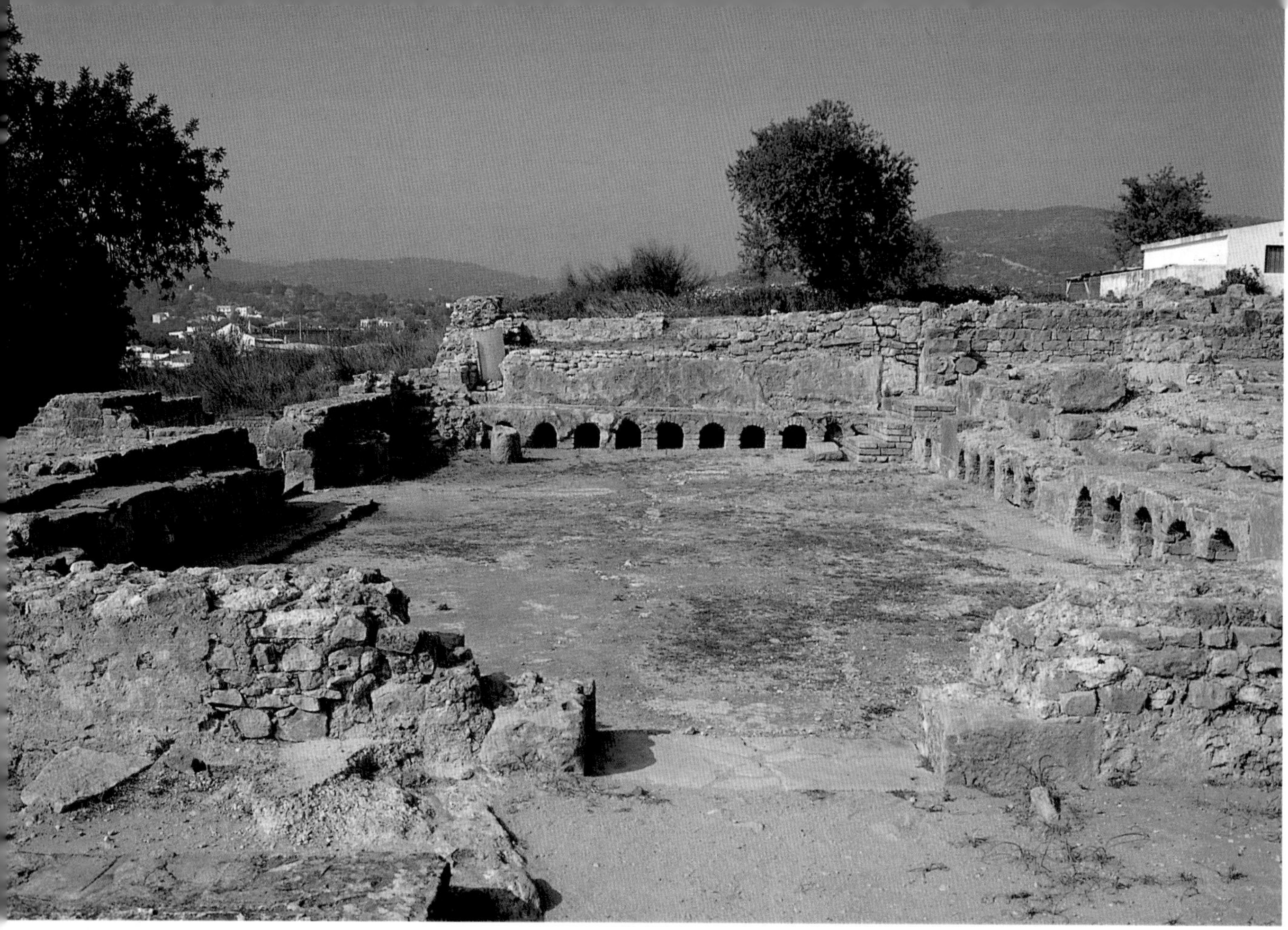

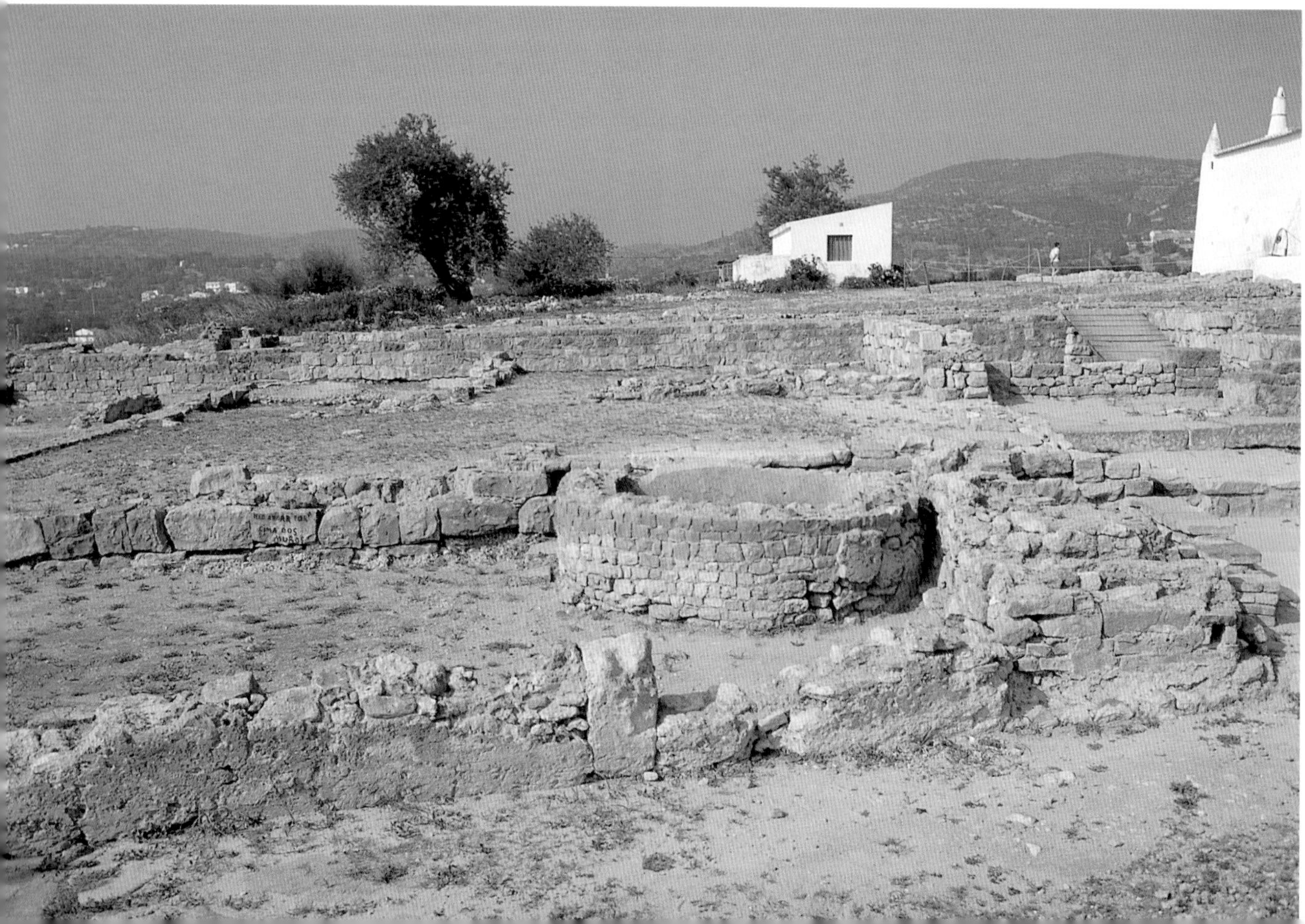

Views of the Temple area

Sunken bath

signs of a vast winery and great tanks for treading the grapes.

The highlight of the house itself is the temple - the sanctuary of water - in the form of a gallery with colonnades ranged round a central cella. The house had paved floors and mosaics lined many of the walls, with geometric motifs and depictions of marine life. Many of the rooms still display wall niches built for the cult of the household gods, the *lares* who protected the home .

Water was channelled to the baths by a highly complex system, evidence of high standards of hydraulic engineering. The large baths are magnificently adorned with finely wrought mosaics.

The scale of the farm buildings suggest that this was a major depot for farming produce, which would be despatched to the city of óssonoba and other parts of the empire.

The Romans left a rich archeological record of their years in the Algarve, but of all the sites Milreu is easily the most complete.

For this very reason there are plans to rebuild the walls high enough to give an idea of the space and perspective of the original buildings and the domes-

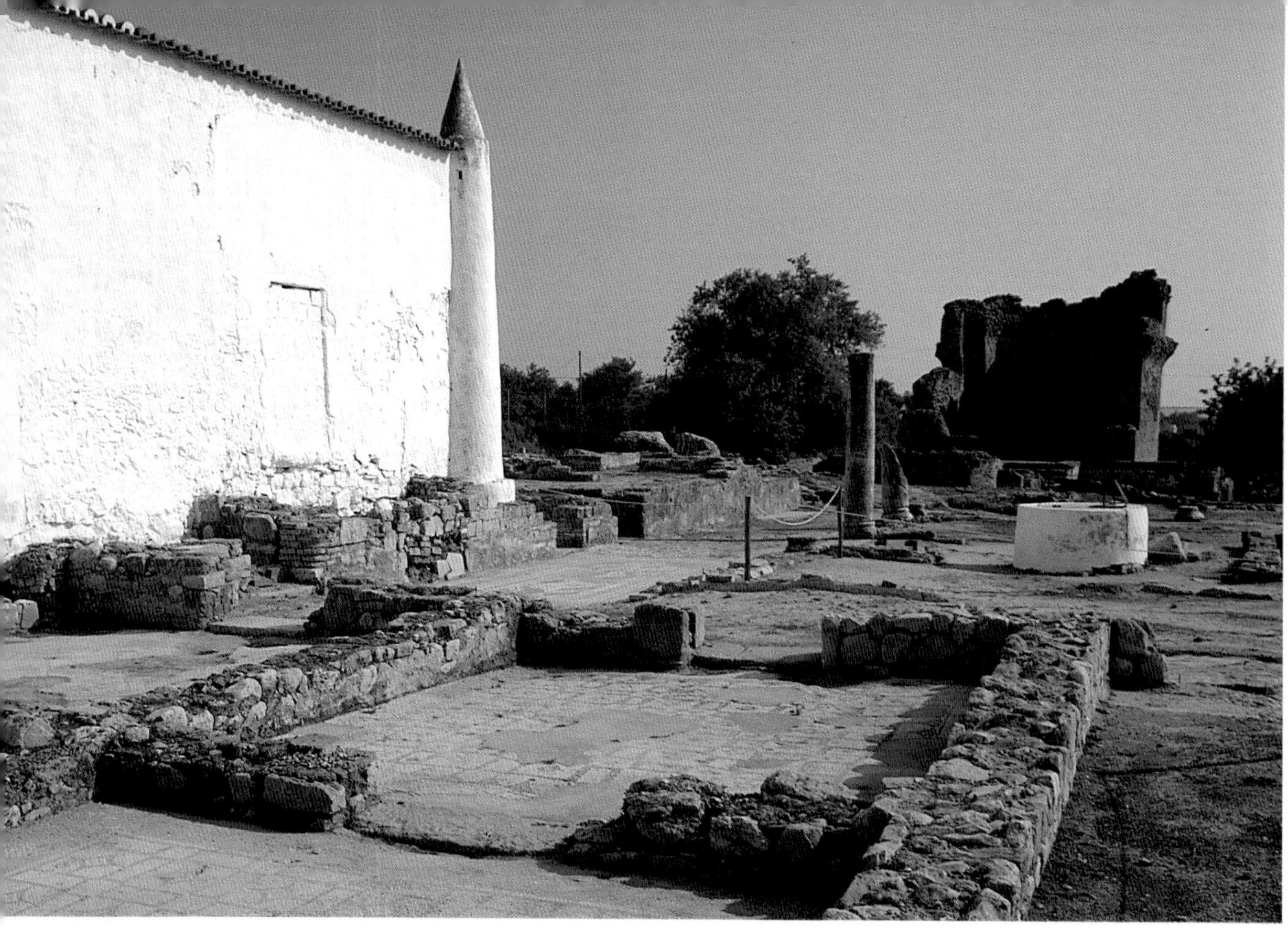

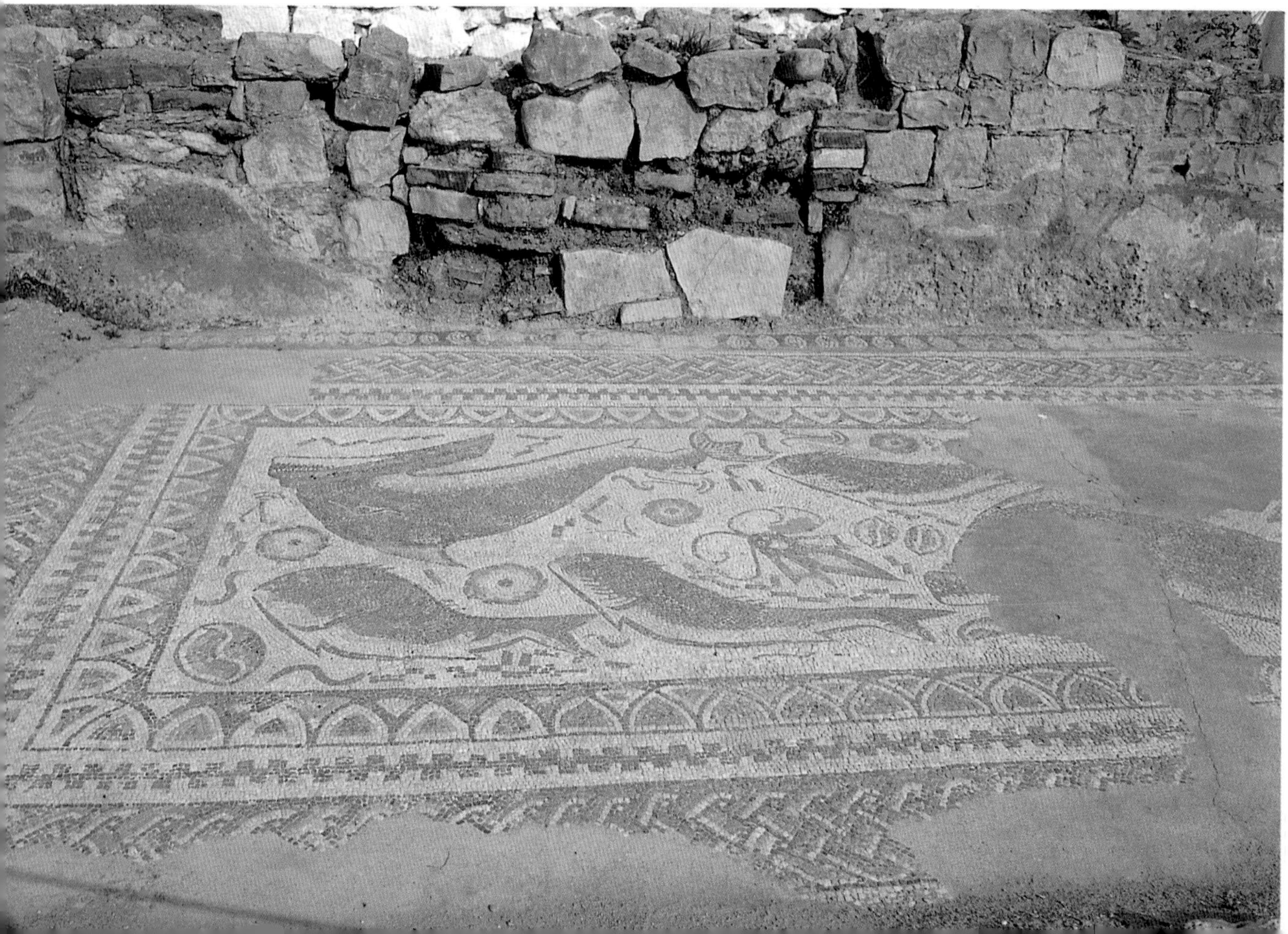

Swimming pool

The Round Tower

Paved floors and mosaics

tic life of those who lived there, without losing the sense of ruins.

Other finds around Milreu means that the total area of archeological interest extends to more than 3 hectares, which would seem to suggest a small settlement around the main farm house. About 880 metres to the north the rains in 1989 washed the mud from the River Seco, revealing a Roman road and the colonnade of a bridge across the river allowing easy travel towards the sea.

Twenty centuries later, Roman Milreu still stands in peaceful countryside, the landscape dotted with almond trees and the heady scent of orange blossom.

ESTÓI

In the last years of the eighteenth century the Counts of Carvalhal came to Estói to build their summer palace. Today, the heavy iron gates are closed, but the public may enter through a simple wooden door into the alley leading to the stables. Gardens stretch from here to the house, with eighteenth and nineteenth century styles competing in exuberance: statues, busts, panels of *azulejo*. Exotic camelia bushes of every colour hide shady corners decorated with Romanesque shale tiles glittering in the sun. The statues of Venus and Diana recline in front of tiled Art Nouveau panels of plants and exotic birds.

The bandstand is all but in ruins, but the busts of the great names of Portuguese literature gaze down unchanged. Among Alexandre Herculano, Luís de Camões, Camilo Castelo Branco and Almeida

The XIX century Parish Church

Balustered stairways at the Estói Palace

The neoclassic palace and part of the neglected gardens

Detail of an azulejos panel

Garret, the face of the Marquis of Pombal makes a surprise appearance, along with the Emperor and Empress of Germany. Palace of enchanted princesses, without the shadows of ancient stone, dungeons and keeps, Estói revels in rustic charms, a retreat from the political turmoil of the court. The lake, stairways and secret bowers conjure up country festivals, tea on the lawn, picnics and hunting trips.

Although the grounds are open to visitors, the 28 rooms of the palace are private. The fine stuc-

Facade of the XVIII century Palace

Fine sculptures decorate the balustered pool of the main terrace

co ceilings and crib can only be glimpsed through the tinted glass of the windows.

Estói did not rise suddenly to greatness when the Counts of Carvalhal chose it for their summer home. Many centuries before, a Roman noble built his villa here, a few hundred metres away in **Milreu.** The remains are the most complete in the country. These archeological finds have fed a fierce war of words between Estói and Faro, both of whom claim the right to the historic name of *Óssonoba*, the main city of the Roman Algarve.

Statues and azulejos panels adorn the garden terraces

The Algarve coastline has always advanced and retreated from the sea. The fact that the coast here has moved some ten kilometres forward is the ground for claims for associating Estói with *Óssonoba*. According to this argument, Faro would have been a modest fishing village, only later developed when the sand islands thrown down at the mouth of the the **Ria Formosa** provided sufficient protection from the sea and the elements.

The pavement of a Roman road was recently discovered north of Estói. This may have been the highway from Castro Marim to Silves. These disputes belonging to the past still make for lively conversation when the locals while away an afternoon in the garden in front of the **Parish Church**, rebuilt in the XIX century, entered by an imposing stairway.

OLHÃO

"Half a century ago, Olhão, swimming in salt and lost to the world, lived only from the sea. Those who were not mariners, were the sons of mariners or the grandsons of mariners. Some were smugglers, whilst some fished off the coast and others fished on the high seas. There was fish a plenty and the life was extraordinary. The boat went to buy in provisions in Almeria or Gibraltar, or sailed up to São Martinho taking figs from the Algarve, coming back with a cargo of apples." This is how the writer Raúl Brandão describes Olhão, a town which the sea seems to have spirited over from somewhere in North Africa. Life here follows a different pattern from elsewhere, in the tangle of streets in the **Bairro da Barreta**, the bustle of the port and the boats in the river mouth.

Some have called this the cubist town, in reference to the white square houses, each topped with a terrace for drying fish or figs, with hardly a tiled roof in sight. In the summer, the kitchen moves out into the street where the sardines, fresh from the fishing

Igreja Matriz

Igreja N. Senhora da Soledade (XVII century)

Repairing the fishing nets

The Municipal Market on the waterfront

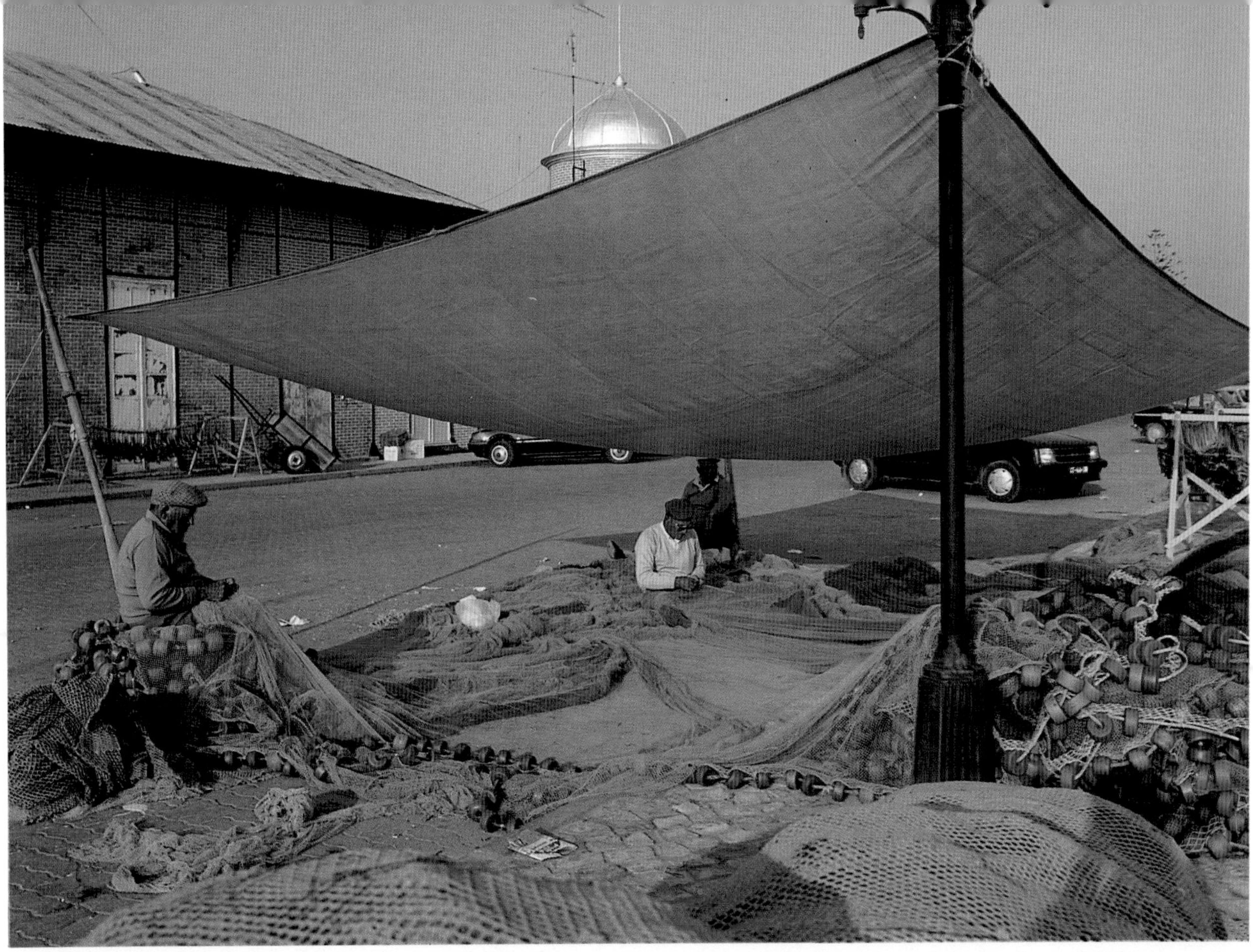

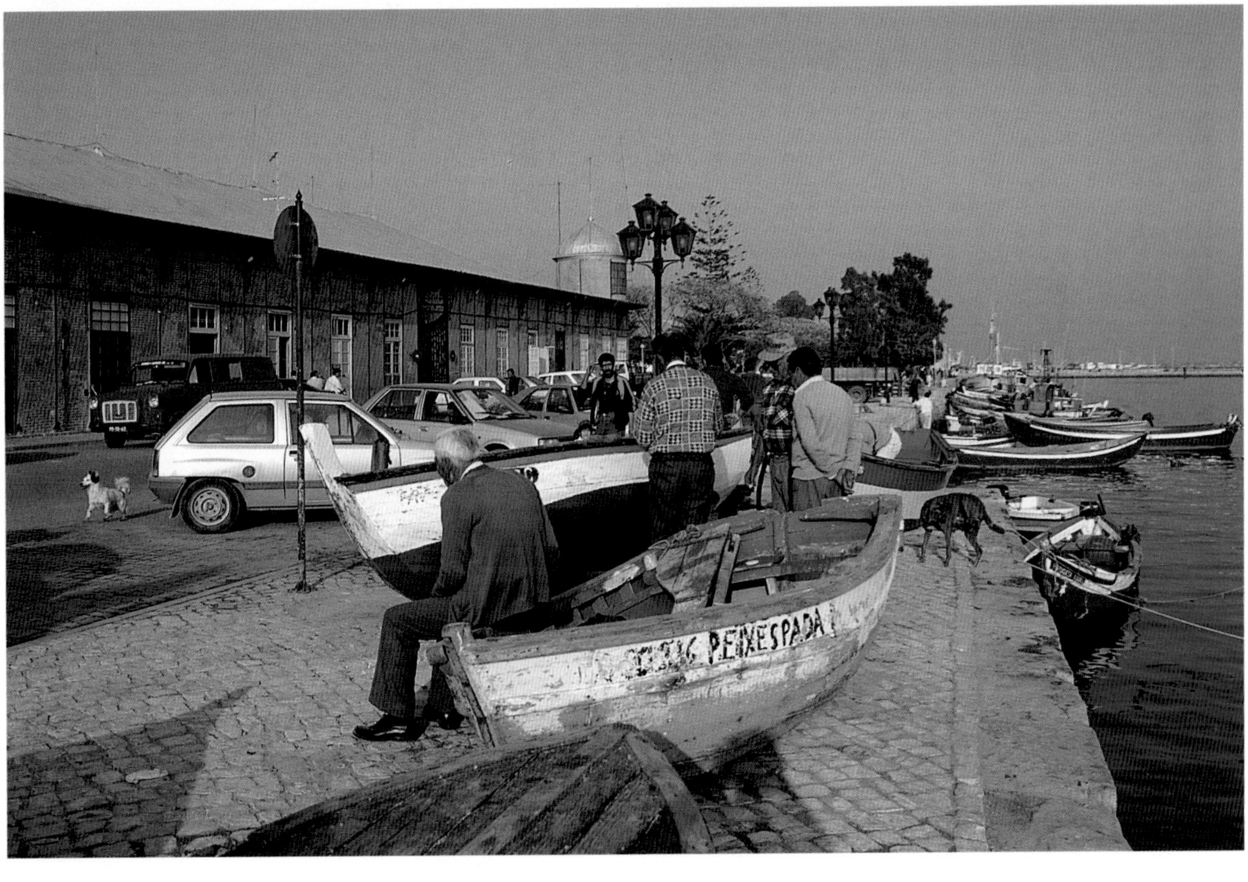
PEIXESPADA

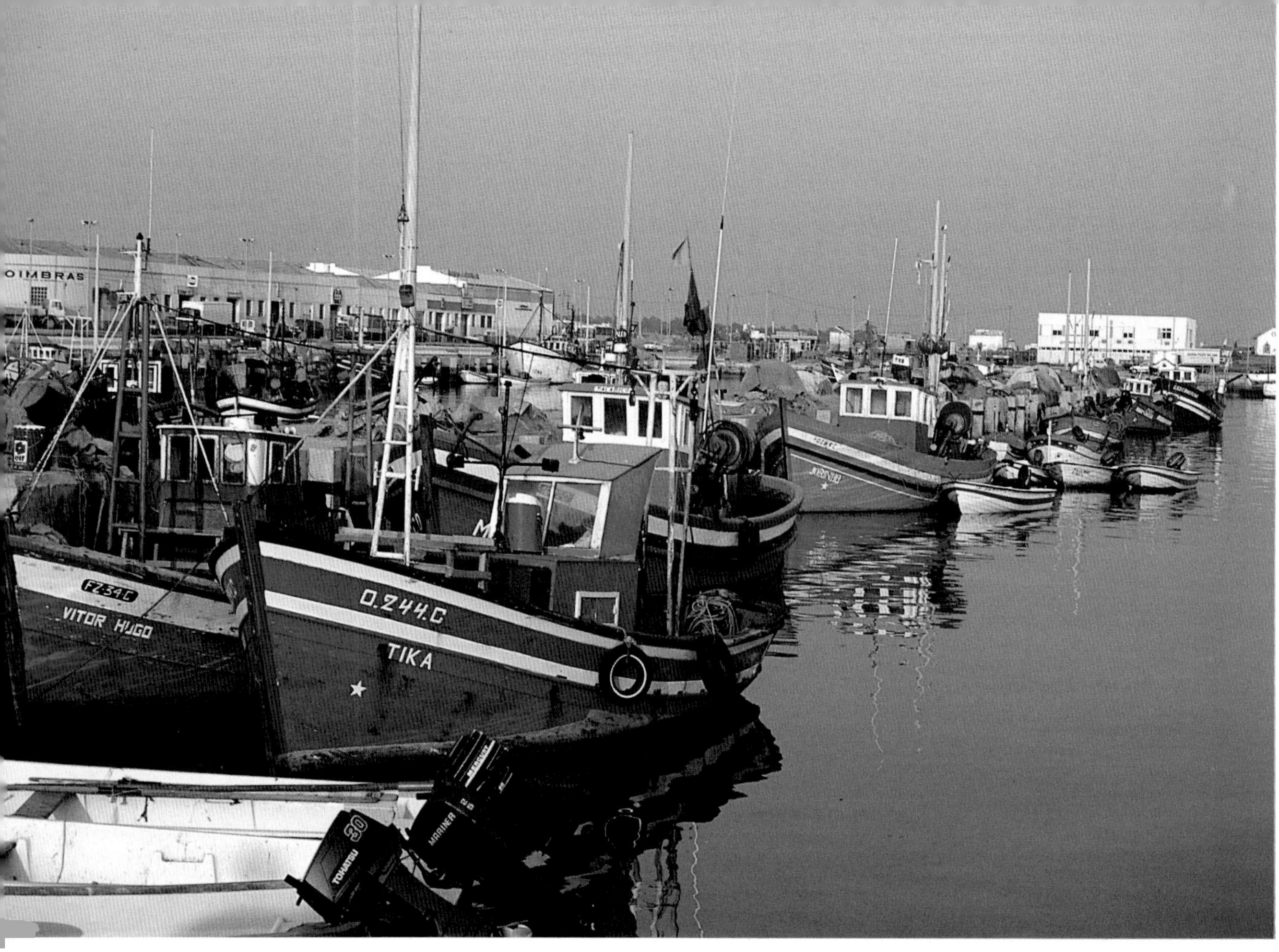
VITOR HUGO
O.244.C
TIKA
MARINER
TOHATSU
30

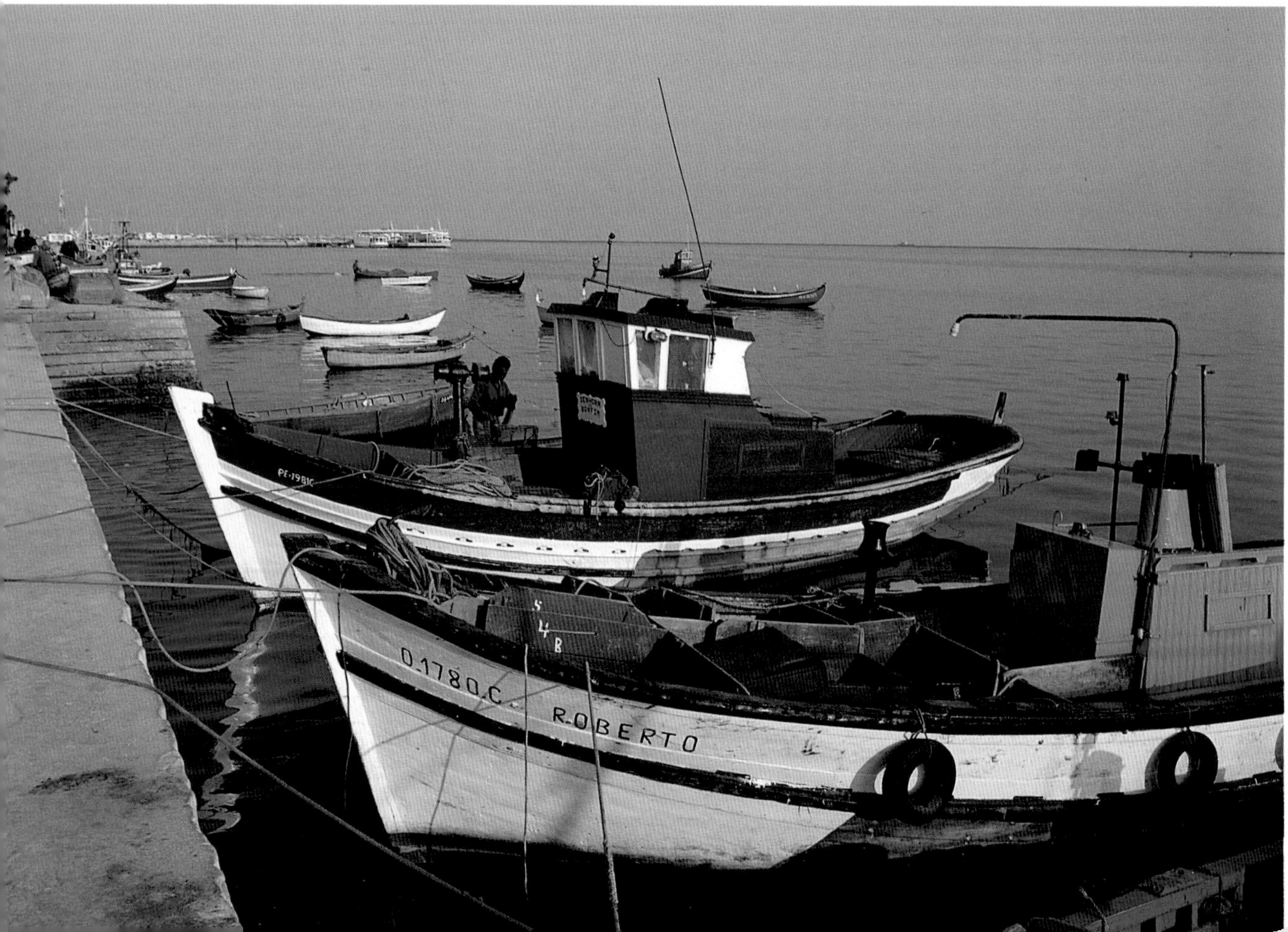
O.1780.C
ROBERTO

Fishing boats and nets

The fishing harbour at Olhão

Drying octopus

nets, cook on charcoal grills. The square houses imprint their style on neighbouring villages, such as Moncarapacho, Fuzeta, Armona and Alfandanga.

With the arrival of fish processing plants life is changing, but it continues to revolve around fish and the sea.

The **Parish Church** has the distinction of having been built with the money of the local fishing community, in the XVIII century; its rich treasures include a painting of Christ. From the bell tower, in the style of an Arab minaret, the view extends over the whole town and the entrance to the port.

Sandy islands stretch out in front of Olhão, as if put there to defend the town. The sand beaches go as far as the eye can see, washed by a crystal clear sea. Small pools abound with marine life, and small prawns will swim fearlessly up to bathers.

The fishermen of Olhão have a precious friend in the Algarve water dog, which has webbed feet and is happy to swim and dive. The origins of the race are unknown, but there is no end to the stories of fishermen who owe him their lives, or their good fortune - the dog dives to depths of 4 metres and guides the fish into the net.

TAVIRA

Seen from a distance the spires of Tavira's 36 churches give a first indication of the town's rich artistic heritage, along with the castle which dominates the river Gilão. The hipped roofs, shaped like treasure chests, carry on an ancient tradition, and in many streets there are still windows with Gothic frames which date back to the Middle Ages.

To some extent stuck in time since the channel which used to lead to the sea silted up, Tavira comes as a pleasant surprise to travellers from busier, noisier places.

The **Igreja do Carmo**, noted for the gilded carving on its altar, is one of many religious monuments worth visiting. The **Igreja de Nossa Senhora das Ondas** (Our Lady of the Waves), was named by the sailors who dedicated the church to her, and it holds the gold- and silver-embroidered standard of the Seamen's Association.

The water is warm at the local beaches, and in the countryside the roads twist through vineyards and orange groves which fill the air with their scent.

Igreja de São Paulo

A view of the town

Interior of the XVIII century Igreja do Carmo

Old houses along the Rio Gilão

The Parish Church at Cacela

On a more practical note, the **Tuna Museum** has displays showing the equipment that was used to catch tuna, back in the days when men struggled to haul up the fish by hand into open boats. The traditional technique disappeared in the 70s with the advent of new methods and is now little more than a memory in the history of the Algarve.

CACELA

Perched on the cliff top, Cacela looks out over the **Ria Formosa**, a village where time has stood still. The fort was built over Roman ruins and the church dates from the XII century. In ancient times this must have been an important urban centre, to judge from the defences built by Phoenicians and Romans. Of this illustrious past remains the beauty of the landscape, with spectacular views from the churchyards or the fortress walls. The sand dunes stretch out to the west, and to the east the twisting puzzle of channels and lagoons of the Ria Formosa.

Beach and walls at Cacela

Platibanda (stucco decorated moulding)

A view of the town and Castle

Saltpans at Castro Marim

CASTRO MARIM

It is hard to set a clear line between Castro Marim and the Guadiana. The river banks are disguised by the checkerboard of salt flats, and the houses are built so close to the water that the land on which they stand is all but hidden.

The castle broods high above the city, evoking turbaned Saracens, knights in armour and the old enmity with Castille, many of whose soldiers perished within the stone walls of the fortress.

The hills of the **Serra do Caldeirão** sweep down to the plain, like a picture frame around the town and the fortifications.

Neolithic finds are evidence that primitive man sought refuge here, the only high ground above the marshlands of the river banks. The various peoples who inhabited the Algarve also settled on the site. During the dark years of the Inquisition, as the wind of religious intolerance blew through medieval

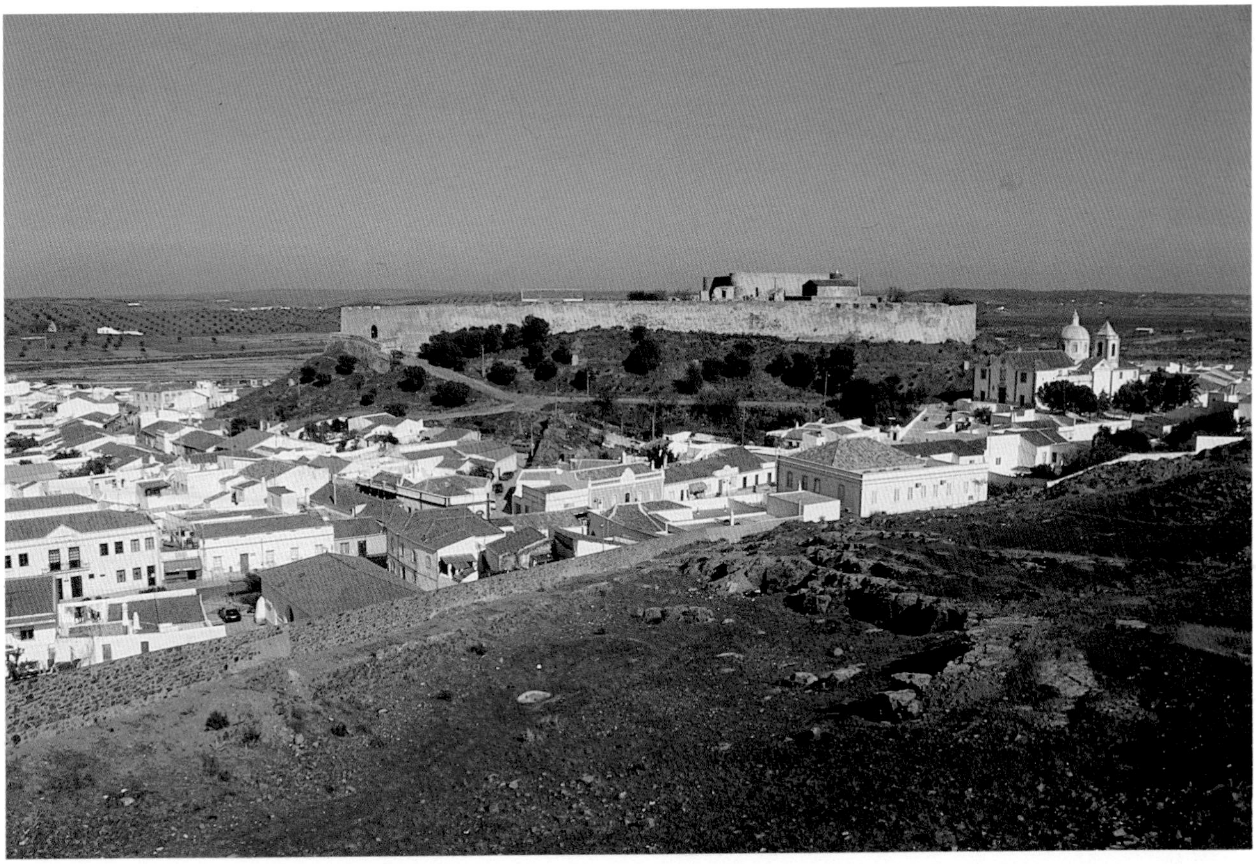

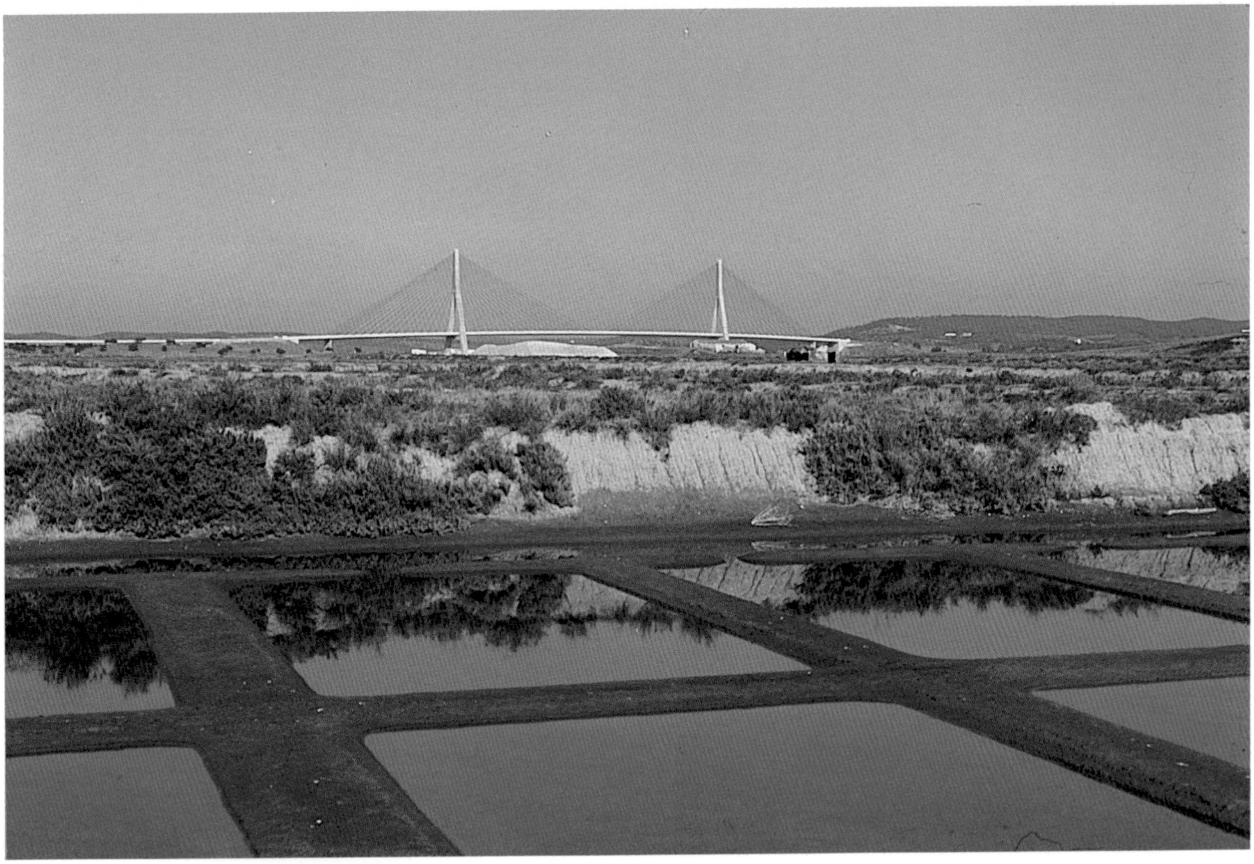

Europe, a penal colony was established, taking advantage of the secure fortifications. In our freer times, an **Archeological and Folk Museum** has opened its doors within the walls, and visitors can walk round the wide defences, dotted with square towers. The view stretches out over the river where the water glistens with fish and sea birds.

MONTE GORDO

For centuries no more than a fishing port, Monte Gordo's long sandy beaches fringed by cool pine woods have thrust it to international tourist fame. The calm and silvery sea and the brightly coloured fishing boats, still laid up on the beach, complete the resort's appeal.

At night the **casino** throbs with its colourful show and the excitement of the roulette wheel. Meanwhile, down by the still waters of the bay, the fishermen light the lamps on their boats and sail out for another rich trawl of shellfish.

Fishing boat

The vast sandy beach at Monte Gordo

VILA REAL DE SANTO ANTÓNIO

The original town of Santo António de Arenilla, built by fishermen on a sand bar in the river Guadiana, was swept away in a violent storm. It would probably have been a typical cluster of white-walled houses, much like Ayamonte, which stands on the opposite bank of the river, in Spain.

With the same determination he showed in rebuilding Lisbon after the earthquake of 1755, the Marquês de Pombal decided in 1774 to raise a new Santo António from the ruins of the old. Nearly a century after the original settlement was destroyed Vila Real de Santo António was built. It took just five months. The town, laid out in a grid design drawn up by the architect Reinaldo Serrano recalls the Baixa quarter of Lisbon. At its heart lies the old **Praça Real**, a model of classical harmony and proportion. The square is paved in the traditional Portuguese style, with a circular pattern that frames the obelisk erected in honour of the town's founder. Once rebuilt, Vila Real soon reestablished itself as a fishing port and went on to become a thriving centre for trade with neighbouring Andalusia.

Craftsman at work

The Parish Church on Praça Marquês de Pombal

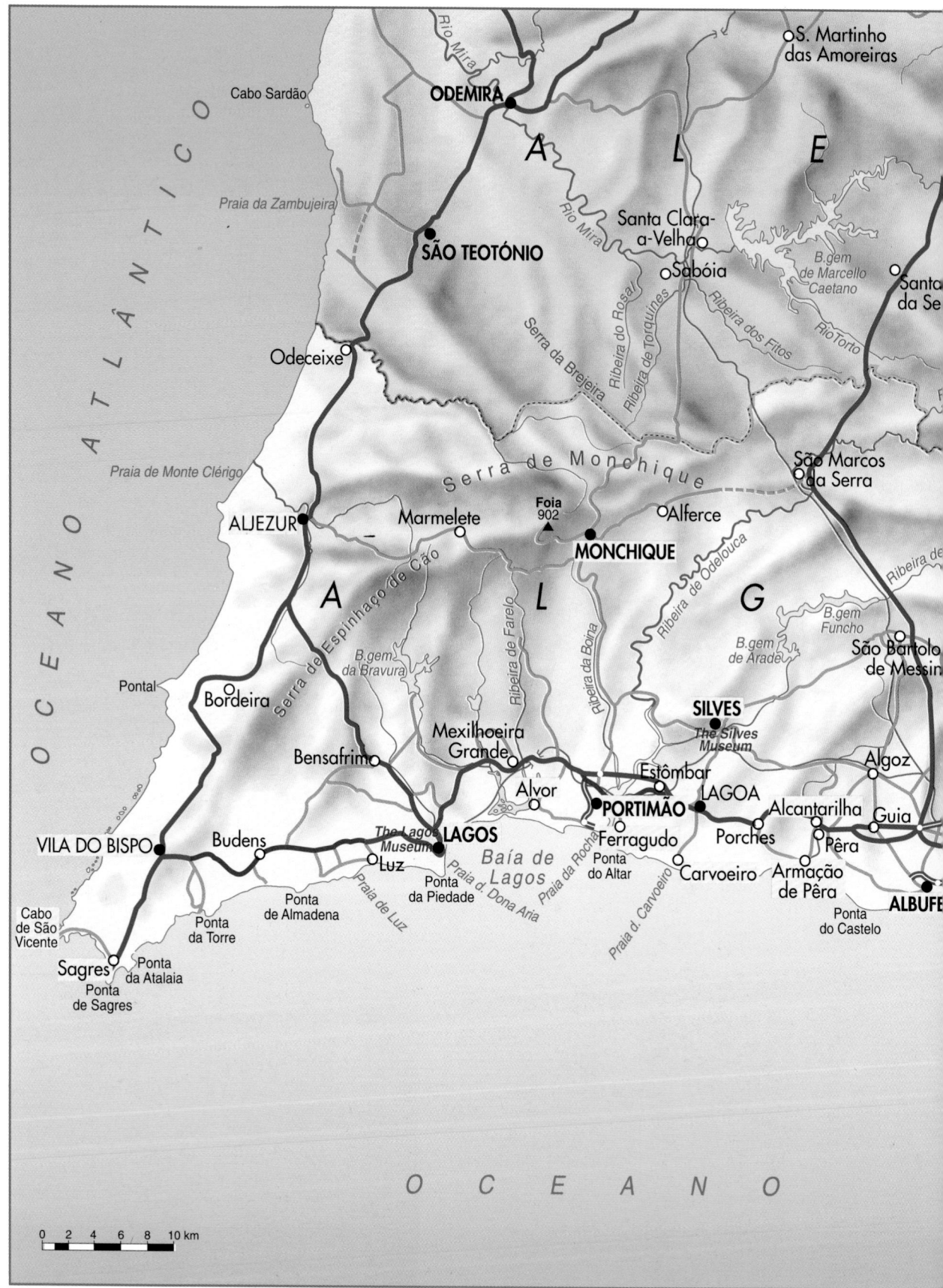

S. Martinho
das Amoreiras

Cabo Sardão

ODEMIRA

Rio Mira

A   L   E

Praia da Zambujeira

Rio Mira

Santa Clara-
a-Velha

SÃO TEOTÓNIO

Sabóia

*B.gem
de Marcello
Caetano*

Santa
da Se

Serra da Brejeira

Ribeira do Rosal

Ribeira de Torquines

Ribeira dos Fitos

Rio Torto

Odeceixe

S e r r a   d e   M o n c h i q u e

São Marcos
da Serra

Praia de Monte Clérigo

ALJEZUR

Marmelete

Foia
902

Alferce

MONCHIQUE

Ribeira de Odelouca

Ribeira de

A

Serra de Espinhaço de Cão

L

Ribeira de Farelo

Ribeira da Boina

*B.gem
de Arade*

G

*B.gem
Funcho*

São Bartolo
de Messin

Pontal

*B.gem
da Bravura*

SILVES
*The Silves
Museum*

Algoz

Bordeira

Mexilhoeira
Grande

Estômbar

Alcantarilha

Guia

Bensafrimo

Alvor

LAGOA

Porches

Pêra

*The Lagos
Museum*

LAGOS

PORTIMÃO

Ferragudo

Carvoeiro

Armação
de Pêra

ALBUFE

VILA DO BISPO

Budens

Luz

*Baía de
Lagos*

Ponta
do Altar

Praia da Rocha

Praia d. Canvoeiro

Ponta
do Castelo

Ponta
da Piedade

Praia d. Dona Ana

Ponta
de Almadena

Praia de Luz

Cabo
de São
Vicente

Ponta
da Torre

Sagres

Ponta
da Atalaia

Ponta
de Sagres

O   C   E   A   N   O

O C E A N O   A T L Â N T I C O

0   2   4   6   8   10 km

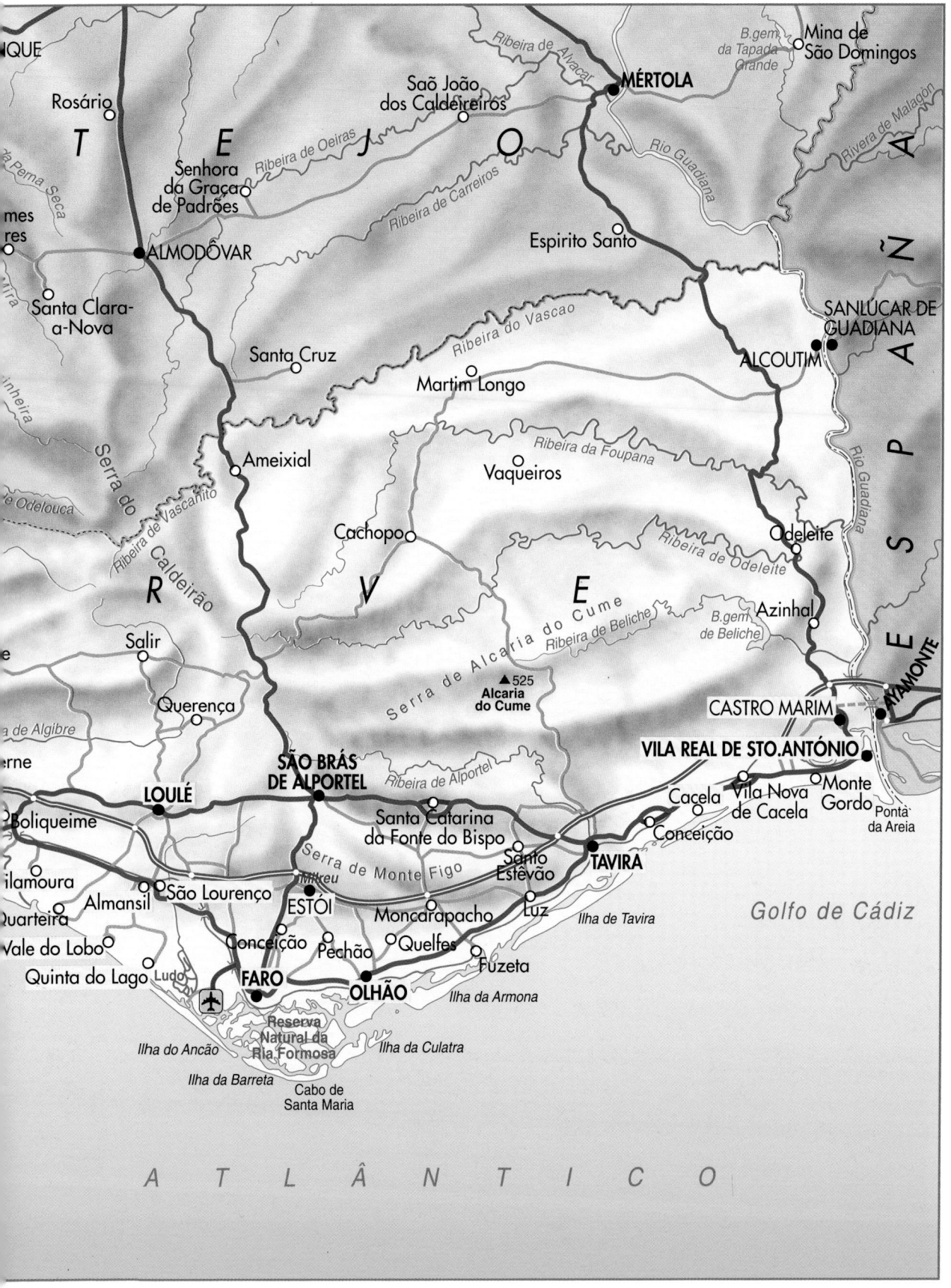

INDEX